The Decade of the 2000s

Cultural Milestones of the 2000s

The Decade of the 2000s

Cultural Milestones of the 2000s

Other titles in *The Decade of the 2000s* series:

The Decade of the 2000s

Cultural Milestones of the 2000s

By Craig E. Blohm

ReferencePoint Press®

San Diego, CA

© 2014 ReferencePoint Press, Inc.
Printed in the United States

For more information, contact:
ReferencePoint Press, Inc.
PO Box 27779
San Diego, CA 92198
www.ReferencePointPress.com

LIBRARY OF CONGRESS CATALOGING-IN-PUBLICATION DATA

Blohm, Craig E., 1948-
  Cultural milestones of the 2000s / by Craig E. Blohm.
    pages cm. -- (Decade of the 2000s series)
  Includes bibliographical references and index.
  ISBN-13: 978-1-60152-524-6 (hardback)
  ISBN-10: 1-60152-524-9 (hardback)
  1. United States--History--21st century. 2. United States--Social conditions--21st century.
  I. Title.
  E902.B57 2014
  973.93--dc23
                                                                        2013017893

Contents

Important Events of the **2000s**

2002
- Euro enters circulation
- Terrorists attack Bali tourist district in Indonesia
- Dwarf planet Quaoar is discovered
- *American Idol* debuts on Fox network
- Xbox Live revolutionizes online gaming

2004
- Hundreds of thousands die in Indian Ocean tsunami
- *Spirit* and *Opportunity* rovers explore surface of Mars
- Facebook is launched
- Hundreds die when Chechen separatists take over a school in Russia
- Palestinian leader Yasser Arafat dies
- Green Belt Movement founder Wangari Maathai of Kenya wins Nobel Peace Prize

2000
- Dire warnings of Y2K Millennium Bug fizzle
- Dot-com bubble bursts
- Israel withdraws all forces from Lebanon
- Dashboard GPS devices become widely available
- Tiger Woods becomes youngest golfer to win Grand Slam
- USS *Cole* is attacked in Yemen

2000　2001　2002　2003　2004

2001
- Terrorist attack on United States kills three thousand people
- Apple launches iPod
- World's first space tourist reaches International Space Station
- Film version of first Harry Potter book is released
- Wikipedia is launched
- United States invades Afghanistan
- Netherlands legalizes same-sex marriage

2003
- United States invades Iraq
- Space shuttle *Columbia* disintegrates on reentry
- Human genome project is completed
- Record heat wave kills tens of thousands in Europe
- China launches its first manned space mission
- WHO issues rare global health alert on SARS

2005

- YouTube is launched
- Burst levees flood New Orleans during Hurricane Katrina
- Kyoto Protocol on climate change goes into effect
- National Academies releases human embryonic stem cell research guidelines
- Earthquake devastates Kashmir
- Lance Armstrong wins seventh consecutive Tour de France (later stripped of all titles)

2008

- United States elects Barack Obama, first African American president
- Oil prices hit record high of $147 per barrel
- US Olympic swimmer Michael Phelps wins record eight gold medals
- Islamic militants attack financial district in Mumbai, India
- Universal Declaration of Human Rights marks sixtieth anniversary

2005 2006 2007 2008 2009

2006

- Pluto is demoted to dwarf planet status
- North Korea conducts its first nuclear test
- Saddam Hussein is executed in Iraq
- West African black rhino is declared extinct
- Twitter is launched
- Global warming documentary, *An Inconvenient Truth,* is released

2009

- WHO declares swine flu outbreak an international pandemic
- Mouse genome is fully sequenced
- Michael Jackson dies at his home in California
- World's tallest man-made structure is completed in Dubai
- Large Hadron Collider becomes world's highest-energy particle accelerator
- Widespread match-fixing scandal rocks European soccer

2007

- Mitchell report details rampant PED use in baseball
- Apple debuts iPhone
- Dozens killed and wounded in mass shooting at Virginia Tech
- Arctic sea ice hits record low
- Google Street View is launched
- Prime Minister Benazir Bhutto of Pakistan is assassinated
- Amazon releases its Kindle
- Great Recession, worldwide economic crisis, begins

Milestones: A Measure of Progress

At the center of ancient Rome stood a monument called the Milliarium Aureum, or Golden Milestone. Although its exact location is now lost to the ages, the column marked the center of the Roman Empire and the end point of a vast network of roads that stretched for almost 250,000 miles (402,336 km). At regular intervals along these roads, milestones were placed to allow travelers to track the distance along their journey. These milestones provided a measure of progress—a visual reminder of a person's achievement on his or her journey.

Everyone experiences his or her own personal milestones throughout the journey of life. Birthdays, graduations, marriage, and having children are all examples of life's milestones. For young people, obtaining a driver's license or turning twenty-one are landmarks that signify the advancement toward adulthood. Often celebrated with parties and family gatherings, personal milestones can be festive and joyous occasions.

Milestones of History and Culture

History is also replete with milestones, some of which have forever changed the course of human existence. The Magna Carta, the "Great Charter" presented to the king of England in 1215, was the first challenge to the absolute authority of the monarchy. It became the basis for English common law and inspired American colonists to seek independence from the British Crown. When a young Serbian anarchist named Gavrilo Princip assassinated Archduke Franz Ferdinand of Austria in 1914, it was the spark that touched off World War I, which eventually led to World War II. The latter conflict created another milestone with the development of atomic weapons, which cast the ominous shadow of nuclear annihilation over international relations in the second half of the twentieth century. That threat subsided after 1991, when the Soviet Union collapsed, a historic end to the nation that had exemplified the Communist threat to the United States.

Culture experiences its own milestones. China's Cultural Revolution from 1966 to 1976 aimed to replace the traditional Chinese culture with Mao Tse-tung's Communist ideology. Millions of Chinese citizens suffered under the new regime, which tortured, imprisoned, and killed its opponents. When the Cultural Revolution ended, China

History is replete with milestones. One such milestone, the signing of the Magna Carta in 1215, changed the course of history as will some of the cultural milestones of the 2000s.

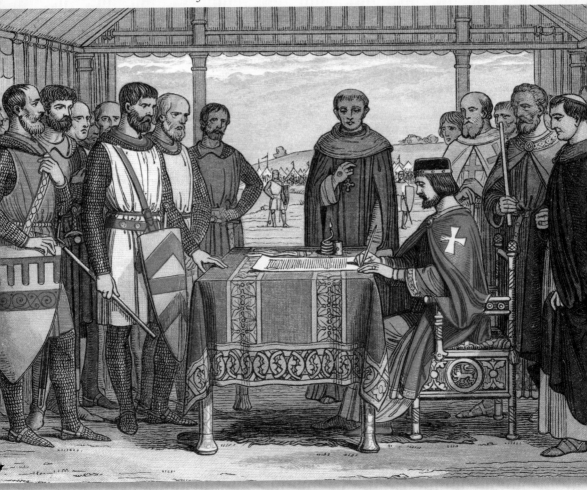

suffered political instability and a weakened economy. Twenty-seven years later, during the Iraq War of 2003, the culture of Iraq received a devastating blow. Numerous museums were ransacked and looted, destroying priceless Iraqi cultural artifacts, works of art, and architecture.

Not all cultural milestones are destructive. For example, several landmark judicial rulings have had a positive impact on society. In *Brown v. Board of Education*, the US Supreme Court ruled in 1954 that establishing separate schools for African American children was unconstitutional. The ruling stated that providing "separate but equal" educational facilities was, in fact, not equal at all and simply furthered racial segregation. Another decision, the 1973 case of *Roe v. Wade*, declared that a woman's right to have an abortion was guaranteed under the US Constitution. Despite the ongoing controversy about this ruling, thousands of women have been spared injury or death by not having to seek back-alley abortions, which were prevalent before *Roe v. Wade*.

Medical milestones have promoted longer and healthier lives. In 1796 Edward Jenner, an English physician, inoculated an eight-year-old boy against smallpox, an infectious disease that was a leading cause of death. The inoculation worked, thus paving the way for the science of immunology that has saved millions of people since the eighteenth century. The first human heart transplant was performed in South Africa by Dr. Christiaan Barnard in 1967. The surgery was experimental and the patient lived only eighteen days, but since then cardiac transplantation has become routine, saving some thirty-five hundred lives each year.

Marking the Journey Through Life

Milestones abound in today's society. In science, architecture, literature, politics, business, and media, milestones are bright spots along the way to the future. On May 10, 2013, construction workers topped off the spire of One World Trade Center in New York. Built near the site where the Twin Towers of the original World Trade Center collapsed following the terrorist attacks of September 11, 2001, the building is the tallest in the Western Hemisphere. New York governor Andrew Cuomo stated,

"This milestone at the World Trade Center site symbolizes the resurgence and resilience of our state and our nation."[1] Its completed height of 1,776 feet (541.3 m) was planned by the architects to symbolize another milestone in US history: the year that the United States declared independence from England.

Rome's Golden Milestone no longer exists; the mile markers along the Roman roads have dwindled to just a few more than a hundred. But each person's own milestones serve as guides through good times and bad. People track their journey through life by remembering the milestones that define their place in culture and in the world.

Chapter ONE

A Changing Society

Evolution is usually understood as a change in biological organisms over an extended period of time. Charles Darwin's theory of evolution explains how living things can adjust in response to changes in their environment. Some species adapt and evolve, while others eventually die out. Societies can also evolve. What was once considered the norm can, in the span of a few decades, seem outdated and archaic. For example, people dressed differently in the early twentieth century than they do today. Then, men wore suits and ties to baseball games, and women's beachwear covered up more than it revealed. Today casual clothing is worn everywhere from the workplace to the house of worship, and ladies' swimwear is barely distinguishable from underwear.

The mores and values of society are changing at an ever-increasing pace as new generations are born and world events affect a globe that seems smaller thanks to the Internet and nonstop media coverage. In the first decade of the twenty-first century, institutions such as marriage, the church, and national security underwent radical, and sometimes devastating, evolution.

Connecting Without Being There

In the not-so-distant past, people got together to socialize by going out with friends to a movie, a dance, a sporting event, or just casually hanging out at someone's home. In the 2000s the Internet changed that to a remarkable degree. From its inception, the Internet had opened up a vast world of information, entertainment, and cybershopping to anyone with a computer and a telephone line. Entranced with the power of the Internet, many people wanted to do more with it.

In 2002 computer programmer Jonathan Abrams began developing a social networking site as a way to meet girls. He named the site Friendster and launched it online in March 2003. By that fall Friendster had 3 million registered users, who created their own personal profiles, sent friends messages, and gathered in virtual communities. "It's networking in a very fun way,"[2] commented artist Sharon Englestein, who used Friendster to connect with fellow artists.

Myspace, a rival networking site, was created in 2003 by two Southern California tech company employees who were also Friendster members. Initially aimed at artists, musicians, and other creative types, Myspace soon began to attract teenagers and young adults and quickly became an international phenomenon that eclipsed Friendster in popularity. Myspace had 100 million accounts by 2006 and was, at its peak, worth $12 billion.

While youth flocked to Myspace, many adults were baffled by the social network's popularity. As one exasperated father complained, "I am so tired of trying to peel my daughter away from the computer on a sunny Saturday afternoon; this whole MySpace craze is out of control!"[3] Myspace parties became a new way for teens to get together, cybernetically, if not physically. Several users would log on to Myspace and surf others' pages, gossiping about those who were not part of the group. But such seemingly innocent online activity led to a new and sinister aspect of social media: cyberbullying.

Sending someone threatening messages, posting harmful or false information about a person on a networking site, and revealing a person's embarrassing or private details are all forms of cyberbullying. About 20 percent of students in a 2011 worldwide study reported being bullied online. For some victims, the consequences can be tragic. In the summer of 2006, Rachael Neblett, a seventeen-year-old high school student in Mount Washington, Kentucky, began to receive anonymous threatening messages through her Myspace account. Throughout the summer the hostile messages continued, culminating in an ominous threat in October: "I am not going to put you in the hospital, I am going to put you in the morgue."[4] Shortly after she received this message, Rachael committed suicide.

The Birth of Facebook

Despite Myspace's tremendous popularity, another site would surpass it to become the largest social media destination in the world. In 2004 Mark Zuckerberg was a sophomore at Harvard University, majoring in psychology and computer programming. Zuckerberg came up with the idea of an online "face book," a visual student directory. The program, initially named Thefacebook, was similar to Friendster and Myspace but limited to Harvard students. Soon, however, it became so popular that Zuckerberg began adding other colleges and universities. Eventually, Thefacebook included high school students; ultimately, anyone over age thirteen could join. In 2005 the site simplified its name to Facebook, and by the next year it had 12 million members. Over the next several years, growth of the site continued to explode, pushing Myspace to a distant second in the social media world.

On October 4, 2012, Zuckerberg announced a milestone on his Facebook page: "This morning, there are more than one billion people using Facebook actively each month. Helping a billion people connect is

The social networking site Facebook transformed how people connect with friends, relatives, and others with shared interests. It remains the world's most popular social networking site.

amazing, humbling and by far the thing I am most proud of in my life."[5] One in seven people throughout the world were using Facebook in 2012. If Facebook were a nation, it would be the third largest in the world.

The Twitter Revolution

While people were gathering together on Facebook, another site was emerging. Twitter, launched in March 2006, was a social networking microblogging site. Twitter messages, or tweets, are limited to 140 characters or fewer. As founder Jack Dorsey explained, "We came across the word 'twitter,' and it was just perfect. The definition was 'a short burst of inconsequential information,' and 'chirps from birds.' And that's exactly what the product was."[6]

People could not resist the lure of dashing off brief tweets for any reason, or none: In 2008 some 400 million tweets were posted. Most tweets are innocuous thoughts and opinions by teens and young adults. But Twitter had a hand in global politics. According to journalist Doug Gross, "Twitter has also been a crucial tool for revolutionaries in Iran, Egypt and elsewhere. It's been used to mobilize relief efforts and raise millions for charitable causes."[7] During the 2009 Green Revolution in Iran following the election of Mahmoud Ahmadinejad, protesters used Twitter to coordinate their activities and provide instant updates as the situation unfolded. The protest even acquired a nickname: the Twitter Revolution.

Social networking, led by Internet giant Facebook, changed the way people share and communicate. It allows people of different backgrounds, nationalities, and cultures to connect in a way never before possible. Zuckerberg wrote, "I'm trying to make the world a more open place."[8] That he succeeded is obvious.

Same-Sex Marriage

Midnight may have been an odd time for a wedding, but at 12:01 a.m. on April 1, 2001, four couples took their marriage vows at city hall in Amsterdam, Netherlands. Amsterdam mayor Job Cohen, who officiated at the ceremonies, told the couples, "There are two reasons to rejoice; you are celebrating your marriage, and you are also celebrating your right to be married."[9] It was a historic occasion because the four couples—three male and one female—were the first same-sex couples in the world to be legally married. Netherlands, traditionally a liberal nation, was at the forefront of a radical and controversial movement in world culture.

The idea that marriage is between a man and a woman can be found as far back as biblical times. In the book of Genesis, God decreed, "Man shall leave his father and mother and be joined to his wife, and they shall become one flesh."[10] The rituals and traditions of marriage have changed throughout history. People have married for many reasons: for love, for political advantage or financial gain, to guarantee the continuation of a family's name, or simply to assure the survival of the human race. As early as the twelfth century, the sacred aspect of marriage was recognized, and in 1563 it officially became a sacrament in the Roman Catholic Church. Although in a few cultures same-sex relationships were accepted, the norm was a one man–one woman marriage.

Many gay couples simply lived together without being married. In the United States they were not entitled to the legal benefits the government extends to married couples, such as income tax breaks, certain Social Security benefits, and employment benefits that apply to one's spouse. In a nation that prides itself in promoting equal rights under the law, gay couples felt they were being discriminated against.

By the late 1990s civil unions began to gain acceptance in many nations. A civil union is a legally recognized partnership between two people, including gay couples. Denmark was the first country to recognize civil unions in 1989; France, Germany, and several Scandinavian countries soon followed. In the United States, Vermont began recognition of civil unions in 2000, the first state to do so. But civil unions were not marriages, and same-sex couples still wanted the social recognition and tangible benefits that came with matrimony.

The Massachusetts Decision

In November 2003 the Massachusetts Supreme Judicial Court ruled that same-sex couples could marry. In the court's opinion, Chief Justice Margaret H. Marshall wrote:

> We are mindful that our decision marks a change in the history of the marriage law. For those who choose to marry, and for their children, marriage provides an abundance of legal, financial and

social benefits. In return, it imposes weighty legal, financial, and social obligations. The question before us is whether, consistent with the Massachusetts Constitution, the Commonwealth may deny the protections, benefits and obligations conferred by civil marriage to two individuals of the same sex who wish to marry. We conclude that it may not.[11]

The gay community rejoiced at the news of the Massachusetts decision, but the conservative opposition prepared for battle. An amendment to the state's constitution was proposed that would reaffirm male-female-only marriages. On the national scene, President George W. Bush gave his support to the Federal Marriage Amendment to the US Constitu-

Two Massachusetts couples rejoice at the news of the 2003 Massachusetts Supreme Judicial Court ruling that same-sex couples can marry. The ruling galvanized both supporters and opponents of same-sex marriage.

tion. Like the Massachusetts amendment, it would have banned gay marriages, but on a national level. Both measures failed to gain support. However, there were some conservative victories: In the 2004 elections, eleven states approved amendments to their state constitutions banning same sex-marriage. But with the Massachusetts court decision, the tide was slowly starting to turn. Polls indicated that acceptance of gay unions was increasing: in one 2004 survey, 60 percent of respondents said they supported either civil unions or same-sex marriages.

By August 2013 same-sex marriage was legal in twelve states and the District of Columbia, as well as in fifteen countries worldwide. Although attitudes have been slowly changing since the first gay marriages in Netherlands, opposition still exists. In the United States the Defense of Marriage Act, which went into effect in 1996, is a federal law that defines marriage as being between a man and a woman. This denies same-sex couples more than one thousand federal benefits available to those in heterosexual marriages. While many liberal churches embrace gay relationships, the Catholic Church and the majority of conservative denominations remain faithful to the biblical standard of a one man—one woman marriage. But there is optimism within the gay community, and those who are committed to legalizing same-sex marriage will continue the fight for its wider acceptance. Anne-Marie Thus, who married Helene Faasen in that historic midnight ceremony in Amsterdam, is one of those fighters. "We were lucky that others had taken up the fight and made it possible for us to get married," she said on their tenth wedding anniversary. "If other people need us now, especially in countries where it is not yet legal, we want to be there for them."[12]

A Decade of Intolerance

"I didn't know I wasn't an American until I was sixteen and in handcuffs."[13] With those words, Adama Bah relived the prejudice and injustice she endured in the wake of the September 11, 2001, terrorist attacks on the United States. On March 24, 2005, Bah and her family awoke to FBI and Homeland Security agents pounding on their apartment door. Bah was handcuffed and taken away for interrogation. The sixteen-year-old was accused of being a terrorist because of an unsubstantiated claim that her name was on a list as a suicide bomber.

Although Bah was not a terrorist, she spent six and a half weeks at a juvenile detention facility, suffering through daily strip searches and cruel taunting by guards. After her release, Bah found it hard to resume a normal life. "I still live in constant fear of federal agents taking me or any of my family members. They did it when I was innocent, and they could do it again."[14]

Fear, Blame, and Hatred

Islam is the world's second-largest religion, with more than 1.6 billion adherents worldwide as of 2010. The vast majority of Muslims are peaceful people who follow the teachings of their holy scripture, the Koran. But after the 9/11 attacks were carried out by a group of radical Muslims backed by terrorist organization al Qaeda, Islam was thrust to the center of the world's attention. Immediately after 9/11, Bush declared a "war on terror," a global military action to eliminate al Qaeda and other terrorist organizations. At home, the war centered on finding potential terrorists on American soil; its targets were mostly Muslims. In October 2001 the USA PATRIOT Act became law, giving US law enforcement agencies greater power in their search for suspected terrorists. According to a report issued by the Council on American-Islamic Relations, in the months after 9/11 more than twelve hundred Muslim men were imprisoned with no way to contact their families or obtain legal representation. But while federal agents were arresting many suspects, they were finding few terrorists. "Thousands were detained in this blind search for terrorists," said Georgetown University law professor David Cole, "without any real evidence of terrorism, and ultimately without netting virtually any terrorists of any kind."[15]

While the government was detaining Muslims, ordinary citizens were becoming wary of Islam and were confused about its teachings. Many Americans blamed the entire religion for the act of a small group of extremists. Soon that blame turned to hatred, discrimination, and even violence. The FBI recorded a 1,600 percent increase in violent acts against Muslims. Near Detroit a forty-five-year-old man from Yemen was shot to death by a man who told him, "I'm going to kill you for what happened in New York and DC."[16] Mosques, Muslim houses of worship, suffered numerous acts of vandalism. In Columbus, Ohio, vandals broke into a mosque and destroyed copies of the Koran, then broke water pipes to create further damage to the building. In other cities mosques were set on fire and damaged by gunshots or by vehicles crashing into them. In Bridgeview, Illinois, a mob of about three hundred young people descended on a local mosque, shouting slogans such as "Death to the Arabs." The protesters flaunted their patriotism by "going back and forth with flags waving from the top of their cars or trucks,"[17] reported an eyewitness.

Even as the hate crimes and violence subsided in the years after 9/11, there remained an atmosphere of suspicion and distrust toward Muslim

PERSPECTIVES

The Myth of Muslim Backlash

In the wake of the September 11, 2001, terrorist attacks, the media were flooded with stories of retaliation against innocent people who were targeted simply because they had a Muslim-sounding name or wore Muslim religious attire. As numerous as these articles and television news reports were, some people questioned whether Muslims were actually being persecuted. Jonathan S. Tobin, senior online editor of *Commentary* magazine, claims that there is "virtually no evidence for the increased discrimination against the followers of Islam." On the contrary, Tobin believes that, in America, Muslims find a society welcoming them "with open arms."

> Those who make these false claims argue that law enforcement activities seeking to root out Islamist support for terrorism either abroad or at home constitute a form of discrimination. But such actions, such as the New York Police Department's surveillance of mosques or community centers where Islamists have congregated, are reasonable reactions to a real threat that deserves the attention of the authorities, not the product of arbitrary bias. Nor do they threaten the vast majority of Muslims who are hard working, law-abiding citizens.

> America is not perfect, but it is a far safer place to practice Islam, or any other faith, than almost all Muslim countries, where religious-based discrimination is commonplace and dissent is ruthlessly wiped out. The backlash myth may die hard, but it remains a myth.

Jonathan S. Tobin, "Backlash Against Muslims Growing? Then Why Are Their Numbers Increasing?," *Commentary*, May 3, 2012. www.commentarymagazine.com.

PERSPECTIVES

The Muslim Backlash Is Real—and Ongoing

In August 2012 a Sikh temple in Oak Creek, Wisconsin, was attacked, leaving six people dead. Although Sikhs are not Muslims, police believe the gunman (who died in the attack) was motivated by anti-Muslim sentiments. Sikh men, who traditionally have beards and wear turbans, are often mistaken for Muslims, and like Muslims, they experienced a rise in hate crimes after 9/11. Deepa Iyer, executive director of South Asian Americans Leading Together, describes a climate of prejudice experienced by Muslims, Sikhs, and others in the United States.

> [Anti-Muslim crime] manifests itself in different ways: a mosque blocked for the past two years from being developed in Tennessee; a Bangladeshi cab driver brutally assaulted in New York because his passenger thought he was Muslim; and a mosque in Missouri destroyed by a suspected arson a day after the Oak Creek tragedy. It extends to politicians, such as Rep. Peter King, R-N.Y., holding anti-Muslim hearings and Rep. Michele Bachmann, R-Minn., making unsubstantiated claims that disloyal Muslims are infiltrating our government.
>
> While these sentiments have been described as racism, Islamophobia or xenophobia, they are all related. Our nation was founded on the values of pluralism and religious freedom. A murderous attack like this, targeting a single faith, is an assault on our American ideals, whether those targeted are Muslims, or Sikhs, or Jews, or Christians.

Deepa Iyer, "Post 9/11 Discrimination Must End," *USA Today*, August 9, 2012. http://usatoday30.usatoday.com.

Americans. Agents of the Transportation Security Administration, the government agency responsible for airline security, continued to detain some travelers based solely on their appearance. Muslim women who wore the traditional garb of their religion were often harassed, some even losing their jobs for refusing to remove their hijab, or head scarf. A poll conducted in 2010 revealed that Americans are more than twice as likely to feel prejudiced against Muslims as against any other major religion. This is despite the fact that two-thirds of Americans admit to knowing little or nothing about Islam. And the problem is not only an American one. As more Muslims immigrate to European countries, incidents of prejudice increase there as well.

Islamophobia is a word often used to denote an unfounded fear or intolerance toward Muslims or Islam. The 9/11 terrorist attacks that began the 2000s gave some people justification for their Islamophobia. Ray Hanania, an Arab American journalist, gives insight into this atmosphere of intolerance:

> I saw how easily people resorted to stereotyping and hatred as a means of dealing with this tragedy. In the weeks after September 11, a man who identified himself by name and said he was one of my neighbors was among hundreds of people who sent e-mails threatening my life. What does it say about a society when someone can feel comfortable in their hatred with no fear of punishment?[18]

Priests and Sexual Abuse

It was a problem that had existed for years, covered by the darkness of shame and secrecy. But in 2002 the *Boston Globe* shone a light on that darkness when it published a series of articles revealing a horrifying secret: for decades Roman Catholic priests had been sexually molesting young boys, and the church had been covering up the shocking transgressions.

Typical of the stories that the *Globe* revealed was that of Christopher Fulchino. As a thirteen-year-old in Weston, Massachusetts, Christopher was abused by his parish priest, John Geoghan, in 1989. On a pretext of having a snack of milk and cookies, Geoghan invited Fulchino to the rectory of St. Julia's parish, where he began to molest the boy. When he finally managed to get free, Fulchino ran out of the room and hid behind the church until his father picked him up. As the boy ran, Geoghan yelled, "No one will ever believe you."[19] Somehow knowing that was true, Fulchino kept the humiliating incident to himself for eight years. When he saw Geoghan on television in 1997 being accused of molesting children, he told his parents what had happened. Only

Boston's Roman Catholic Cardinal Bernard Law (center) prepares for a 2002 deposition in a child sexual abuse lawsuit stemming from the actions of convicted pedophile priest John Geoghan. Throughout much of the 2000s the Church dealt with accusations of shielding priests like Geoghan.

then did he learn that his father also had been molested by a priest almost forty years before.

The sexual abuse of children by Catholic priests has always been an unspeakable act that was kept hidden by both perpetrator and victim. Research conducted as a result of the *Boston Globe* articles revealed that 4,392 priests were alleged to have abused children between 1950 and 2002, with more than ten thousand victims making accusations against priests. Thomas Plante, a psychology professor at Santa Clara University, a Catholic institution, stated that "approximately 4% of priests during the past half century (and mostly in the 1960s and 1970s) have had a sexual experience with a minor."[20]

The response from the Catholic hierarchy was seen by many as inadequate, even criminal. "Some bishops have come forward and given names to prosecutors," commented Gary Hayes, a Catholic priest. "But the church as a whole has responded with arrogance, defiance, ignorance and indifference."[21] In many cases the abusing priests were quietly reassigned to other parishes, where their abusive practices continued. The problem of child abuse by priests was not limited to the United States but was, in fact, a worldwide crisis. Allegations of abuse came to light in Canada, Great Britain, Australia, Brazil, France, and numerous other countries.

For the victims of such abuse the consequences were devastating. Many have struggled with drug and alcohol abuse, psychiatric problems, and lingering feelings of guilt. One account estimates that perhaps 20 percent of abused boys have considered suicide; news reports confirm that many succeeded. The Catholic Church has also suffered because of the scandal. By the end of the decade, the monetary settlements of lawsuits against abusing priests totaled more than $3 billion, and many dioceses were forced into bankruptcy. But the real damage goes beyond money. According to Richard McBrien, a professor of theology at Notre Dame, "This is the greatest crisis in the modern history of the Catholic church. It raises serious questions about the integrity of its priesthood, and the Catholic church just can't function without a priesthood that has the support and trust of its people."[22]

Chapter TWO

Revolution in the Arts

When Johannes Gutenberg created the moveable type printing press around 1450, he began a revolution of the printed word that rapidly spread throughout the world. Printing presses sprang up in major cities all across Europe, producing some 8 million books by the beginning of the sixteenth century. His first and most famous project, known today as the Gutenberg Bible, helped spread the message of Christianity throughout Europe and, eventually, the world.

Gutenberg's printing press dramatically altered the documentation of events, the spread of ideas, and the creative processes that fueled cultural change. The 2000s witnessed a similar transformation in nearly all aspects of the arts. Computers, the Internet, and advanced digital imaging began to influence the way people created and consumed entertainment. New avenues for reading and for viewing movies opened up almost limitless possibilities for consumers. Wizards, witches, werewolves, and vampires became the new heroes and villains of popular literature. The resurrection of 3-D, an old cinema gimmick, sent images virtually flying off theater screens.

But the revolution in the arts also created a new set of rules for those who produced artistic content. Entire industries found themselves fighting for their very survival in a world where the new business model seemed to be adapt or perish.

A New Wave in Music

In the 1950s rock and roll was the latest craze to take the music industry by storm. Big bands and crooners like Frank Sinatra were being eclipsed in popularity by the hip-wiggling gyrations of Elvis Presley and the rocking beat of Bill Haley and the Comets. From car radios, juke boxes, and the new transistor radio, rock and roll blasted its way into popular culture. For teenagers of the era, a trip to the local record store was the only way to own their favorite artists' latest offerings. Record sales soared as teens spent their allowances or hard-earned soda shop wages on the latest 45-rpm vinyl release. The music industry was booming.

Fast forward to 2004. Vinyl records, easily damaged by wear and scratches, had given way to shiny compact discs that provided listeners with crisp, virtually noiseless sound. But if the music was clearer, the future of the music industry was not. Album sales had fallen 31 percent since 2000, with lost revenue estimated at $4.2 billion. By the end of the decade, music sales would plunge by 50 percent. Behind this massive downturn that threatened to devastate the industry was a young man named Shawn Fanning.

Napster and iTunes

Fanning was a nineteen-year-old college dropout in 1999 when he came up with an idea that would forever change the music industry. Fanning knew that "there was a lot of material out there sitting on people's hard drives. So that's the idea, that there's all this stuff sitting on people's PCs—and I had to figure a way to go and get it."[23] What he figured out became Napster, an online file-sharing service. Napster made it possible for users to search for songs stored on any computer and download them directly to their own computer. Thousands of songs were indexed in Napster's servers, which directed users to a computer that contained the requested song. The ease of downloading music files, plus the fact that it was free, made the service an instant hit, especially on college campuses.

Although the main idea behind Napster was to make it easier for people to listen to and share their favorite songs, the new service was soon painted by members of the music industry as a form of piracy. Ron Stone, manager of several popular musicians, expressed this point of view in an interview in 2000. "Napster is the greatest example of aiding and abetting a theft that I have ever seen," Stone said. "Ninety-nine percent of their content is illegal."[24] The more people downloaded music from Napster and similar sites like Kazaa and Grokster, the less money went to record labels and artists. It was not only the music industry that was affected. According to the Institute for Policy Innovation, "The impact of

MP3 players and music downloading forced huge changes in the music industry. Music lovers who traditionally bought whole records or CDs could download individual songs directly to their computers, bypassing traditional record stores entirely.

music piracy flows throughout the U.S. economy. Piracy in one segment of the economy can affect other industries because the economy is an 'interlocking' system. Changes in supply or demand in one industry can and do affect supply and demand in other industries."[25]

Thwarting Music Pirates

With the availability of digital music on such websites as Apple's iTunes, it was inevitable that illegal downloading would soon follow. When Apple created the iTunes Store, it had to license the music it sold from the music companies that owned the copyrights. These companies insisted that songs sold on iTunes include digital rights management (DRM) software to prevent illegal copies from being made. Apple's DRM software, developed in 2003, was called FairPlay, and it allowed songs downloaded from the iTunes store to play only on iPods and other Apple devices.

Backlash against FairPlay and other DRM systems came almost immediately. People felt that since they paid for their music, they should be able to do whatever they wanted with it. It was not long before hackers learned how to circumvent the DRM coding, and they were more than willing to share their methods with the online community. Even Apple CEO Steve Jobs admitted that DRM failed to prevent piracy. "The problem, of course," he wrote, "is that there are many smart people in the world, some with a lot of time on their hands who love to discover such secrets and publish a way for everyone to get free (and stolen) music."

By January 2009 Apple reached a deal with the major music companies and announced that it would remove DRM restrictions from all of its songs in the iTunes store.

Steve Jobs, "Thoughts on Music," February 6, 2007. www.apple.com.

On the brink of disaster, the record industry fought back with a powerful weapon—the lawsuit. In July 2004 Charli Johnson, a University of Kansas student, received notice that she was being sued by the Recording Industry Association of America (RIAA). Her crime, according to the RIAA, was that she illegally shared 592 songs from her computer. Rather than fight the suit, Johnson settled with the RIAA; she agreed to pay the association $3,000—not a small sum for a college student. "The odds were overwhelming against me," said Johnson. "Plus, to me there was never any question I was downloading music. How could I fight that?"[26] Eventually, the RIAA sued more than thirty-eight thousand people of all ages and from all walks of life and took legal action against file-sharing sites. Napster was one of these sites, and it was shut down in 2001.

But the ease of downloading music and the popularity of MP3 players meant that music delivered to the consumer via the Internet was here to stay. The music industry was finally forced to admit this, and the five major record labels signed deals with Apple for distributing their artist's music, thus ensuring that they and their musicians would receive proper royalties. The success of Apple's iTunes Store, which opened in April 2003, proved that people would pay 99 cents for a song by their favorite artist. The industry also began looking to new sources of revenue, such as licensing music for use as cell phone ringtones. Joshua Friedlander, RIAA's vice president of research, remarked in 2010, "There have been a lot of changes over the past 10 years. The industry is adapting to consumers' demands of how they listen to music, when and where, and we've had some growing pains in terms of monetizing those changes. The industry is doing a lot of things that are putting us back on the right track."[27]

The Wizarding World of Harry Potter

At midnight, most young people are safe at home, tucked into their beds and fast asleep. But as that hour approached on July 7, 2000, across the United States, thousands of kids and their parents stood in long lines waiting for stores to open their doors. These drowsy throngs were eagerly awaiting the arrival, not of a new high-tech toy or the latest video game, but the prime example of low-tech media: a book. "People are frenzied out there about this book," commented Richard Klein, co-owner of a bookstore in Huntington, New York. "I have never seen anything like this."[28] The book was *Harry Potter and the Goblet of Fire*, the fourth entry in the wildly popular series about a boy wizard and his friends at the Hogwarts School of Witchcraft and Wizardry.

The book was published simultaneously in the United Kingdom, Canada, and the United States. Scholastic, *Goblet of Fire*'s US publisher, printed an initial run of 3.8 million copies—its largest up to that time. Eventually, more than 66 million copies would be sold worldwide. But *Goblet of Fire* was just a part of the global Harry Potter phenomenon. In all, seven Harry Potter books were published between 1997 and 2007. By 2011 the series had sold 450 million copies and had been translated into sixty-seven languages.

The creator of this elaborate fantasy world, British writer J.K. Rowling, spent seventeen years developing and writing the books, progressing from an out-of-work single mother to the first billionaire author. And while Harry Potter was very good for Rowling, he also exerted an even greater influence: in a world of violent video games, superhero movies, and flashy pop music idols, kids began to read once more.

"Harry Potter really got my daughter reading again," said one mother waiting in a midnight line. "She didn't read books before and now she loves it."[29] Twelve-year-old Caity Richards from Brookline, Massachusetts, said, "I think it's really cool that the whole country's involved. And it's not just U.S.A.—its global. You really feel like you're a part of something."[30] It is nothing short of remarkable when a fictional character can make a young person feel part of a global movement. And while traditionally more girls than boys enjoy reading, Rowling's books have narrowed that gender gap. Bookstore owner Margot Sage-EL said of *Goblet of Fire*, "The most phenomenal thing is that boys who didn't read are devouring this book. And the book seems to have awakened in children a realization that reading is entertainment."[31]

Vampires Arise

While wizards were flying into the young adult's literary world, vampires were taking a bite out of teen reader apathy. And it all began with a dream. In June 2003 twenty-nine-year-old Stephenie Meyer woke up with the memory of a vivid dream she had had during the night. In the dream, two teenagers stood in a meadow talking in the bright sunlight. She was an ordinary girl, while he was a seemingly perfect specimen of young manhood, with one unusual trait: he was a vampire. As Meyer recalled that morning: "I got up and took care of the immediate necessities and then put everything that I possibly could on the back burner. I was so interested in the characters that for the first time since having my oldest son, I sat down at the computer and started writing."[32] After three months of intense sessions at the computer keyboard, Meyer had completed the first draft of the vampire novel that became the best seller *Twilight*.

J.K. Rowling, author of the famed Harry Potter books, autographs the final book in the seven-book series for a costumed fan in 2007. Rowling's imaginative fantasy world and appealing characters attracted millions of readers around the world.

Meyer had written the story for herself, without much thought of getting it published. On the advice of her sister, she contacted several literary agents; by November 2003 Meyer had a publisher. And that publisher had the beginning of a phenomenon to rival Harry Potter. *Twilight* was released in 2005; the book and its three sequels—*New Moon, Eclipse,* and *Breaking Dawn*—sold more than 100 million copies in thirty-seven languages and eclipsed *Harry Potter*'s run on the *New York Times* best-seller list. Fans of the *Twilight* saga lined up at bookstores to await the release of the latest installment, many dressing up as their favorite characters. Many even write *Twilight* "fan fiction," creating their own stories about the characters they have grown to love and posting them on the Internet.

Harry Potter and the Conservative Counterattack

As one of the most spectacular successes in the history of publishing, the Harry Potter books have gained millions of passionate fans all over the world. Young and old alike are captivated by the adventures of Harry and his companions in the magical world created by author J.K. Rowling. But not everyone is a Potter fan. Some people believe that the books promote evil and are harmful to the young readers who have grown to love them.

Much of the opposition comes from evangelical Christians, many of whom believe that the Potter books promote magic and witchcraft. Many detractors have demanded that the books be removed from schools; some have gone so far as to hold book burnings. Pat Robertson, an influential evangelical leader, condemned the books as glorifying the occult on his nationally televised show, *The 700 Club*. But not all Christians are anti-Potter. There are many books written by theologians and ministers that argue that the Harry Potter books are actually based on Christian values and can lead their fans to an understanding of spirituality in the real world.

All this devotion to fictional worlds has had an impact in the real world. Authors like Stephenie Meyer and J.K. Rowling have changed the publishing industry. According to *Time* magazine critic Lev Grossman, Meyer points out that "children are now willing to read 500-page novels, and adults are now willing to read books written for children."[33] And author Jodi Picoult says, "Stephenie Meyer has gotten people hooked on books, and that's good for all of us."[34]

Advances in Cinema

While Harry Potter was flying around his fantastical wizarding world on the pages of Rowling's wildly successful books, filmmakers were creating their own amazing worlds. And in many of these new cinematic worlds, characters and objects seemed to leap from the screen and into the audience. 3-D films were not a new phenomenon in the 2000s, but they had a new impact on an industry that thrives on innovation and spectacle.

The idea of presenting movies as the human eye sees in the real world—where objects are perceived with depth and dimension—dates back to the early twentieth century. But it was not until midcentury that studios began making feature-length 3-D films. By the early 1950s people were staying home watching television rather than going out to their local theaters. One way the studios tried to lure viewers back was by producing movies in 3-D—something that TV could not offer. The experience, while unique, gave many viewers headaches, and the 3-D glasses required to view the effect were uncomfortable. "The technology was too cumbersome," said producer and film historian Bruce Goldstein. "The audiences didn't like the glasses. But it was a big sensation momentarily."[35] Moviegoers soon tired of the gimmick, and 3-D movies vanished.

During a resurgence in the 1980s, the 3-D effect was often used in films produced in the IMAX wide-screen format. With the arrival of digital cinema cameras in the 2000s, 3-D films became easier to produce and looked better on the screen. James Cameron, Oscar-winning director of the blockbuster *Titanic*, became a vocal advocate of 3-D movies. His 2003 documentary *Ghosts of the Abyss* was produced in the IMAX 3-D format, after which he stated, "I'm just going to do everything in 3D now."[36] The list of films that were produced in 3-D continued to grow during the decade, including *The Polar Express* in 2004, the first animated 3-D feature. To capitalize on the growing interest in 3-D, studios began converting many films that originally had been shot in 2-D (including Cameron's *Titanic*) to 3-D for rerelease. And despite the higher ticket cost for 3-D films, movie fans were not dissuaded from attending. "The audience is there," Paul Dergarabedian, an expert in box-office analysis, commented in 2009. "Every time we've seen a movie come out in 3-D or IMAX, we're finding that moviegoers are totally willing to pay the premium."[37]

Creating *Avatar*: 3-D and CGI

Audiences certainly got their money's worth when Cameron's 3-D masterpiece *Avatar*, a visually stunning science-fiction film, was released in 2009. Produced at a cost of $237 million, the film earned more than $2.78 billion worldwide, making it the highest-grossing film of all time. Cameron has set his sights on exporting his vision and enthusiasm for 3-D to Asia. "The future of entertainment is 3-D," he said during a 2012 visit to China, "and we believe the future of 3-D is right here in China."[38]

The on-screen world of *Avatar* was a strange and beautiful place filled with fantastic landscapes and astonishing creatures. But a visitor to the set during filming would have seen none of this. Instead, the soundstage was a vast empty space more reminiscent of the aircraft hangar it had once been than a film studio. Actors performed wearing jumpsuits studded with reflective markers; other markers speckled their faces, giving them the appearance of having blue measles. These markers were used as reference points to record the actors' movements; computers then converted the live actors into the beings seen on-screen (a technique called motion capture). The exotic setting of Pandora, the moon where Avatar took place, and its inhabitants could not have been created without the art form of computer generated images—CGI.

Avatar was not the first film to use CGI. As computers became faster and more powerful in the 1980s and 1990s, computer-generated visual effects progressed from simple wire-frame graphics to realistic backgrounds, animals, and humans. By the 2000s CGI had become a unique art form that was regularly used to create virtual worlds and creatures that would be impossible, dangerous, or prohibitively expensive to build in the real world. Filmmakers' imaginations were no longer bound by reality but could soar to places unimaginable just a few years before. As the popularity of films centering on comic book superheroes such as Superman, Spider-Man, and the Incredible Hulk exploded, so did the use of GCI to render the worlds that these amazing characters inhabited. These films often featured scenes of the destruction of buildings and other structures that would have been impossible without the use of CGI.

Digital Imagery in Animation

Animated films are uniquely suited for CGI. Traditionally, animated films have been created by painstakingly drawing characters on clear acetate cels. Photographing thousands of these cels to show movement is time-consuming and expensive. Computers streamline the animation process, making it more cost-effective by requiring fewer animators. The young audiences at which most animated films are aimed are used to seeing computer-generated figures on their computers. To them, hand-drawn cartoons may seem old-fashioned by comparison.

CGI animation has now mostly replaced hand-drawn cartoons, and the lifelike quality of animated characters improves with each passing year. In 2003 Disney, the creator of the first feature-length animated film, announced that it was abandoning traditional animation in favor of computer animation. In the 2000s audiences flocked to such feature-length animations as *Finding Nemo*, *Cars*, *WALL-E*, and *Up*. Each of these films is an example of the new art of computer animation. While not everyone was happy to see traditional animation eclipsed by digital imagery, the creative freedom and unlimited possibilities of digital production make it hard for innovative filmmakers to resist.

Reaching for the Sky

The United States was once the principal home of skyscrapers—buildings that soared majestically upward to proclaim the might and wealth of the nation. From the late nineteenth century through the twentieth century, America was the home of most skyscrapers. At various times the Empire State Building and World Trade Center in New York and the Willis (formerly Sears) Tower in Chicago all held the title of world's tallest building. But as the new millennium approached, other areas of the world began to overtake the Western Hemisphere in the construction of daring new buildings taller than any that had come before.

On October 17, 2003, Ma Ying-jeou, mayor of the city of Taipei, Taiwan, fastened a golden bolt to the structure of a new skyscraper at the building's topping-out ceremony. This symbolic gesture marked the completion of construction on Taipei 101. When it officially opened in 2004, it was the first "world's tallest building" of the twenty-first century. Towering over Taipei's financial district, at 1,667 feet (508 m), Taipei 101 was also the world's first building to break the half-kilometer mark. As befitting a twenty-first century structure, Taipei 101 features energy-efficient glass curtain walls, satellite Internet access, and aerodynamic elevators, and it is designed to withstand earthquakes and typhoons.

Perhaps more important than technology is the building's symbolism. Taipei 101's shape represents the traditional Chinese architecture of the pagoda, as well as that of the bamboo plant. The design is based on the number *8*, which is considered a lucky number in China. Imbued with such imagery, Taipei 101 makes a statement about how architecture reflects the cultural differences between East and West. According to the building's promotional brochure:

The greatest challenge in designing a statement building is not the construction technology involved, but how the building reflects the culture in which it functions. The spirit of architecture lies in the balance between local culture and internationalism. In the West, a tall building demands respect and attention from the spectators. To the Asians, it symbolizes a broader understanding and anticipation of things to come: we "climb" in order to "see further."[39]

Attaining New Heights

Records are made to be broken, and this holds true for Taipei 101, whose reign as the tallest building in the world lasted only six years. In September 2004, just a few months before Taipei 101 opened to the public, construction began on a skyscraper of a magnitude never seen before. The building, Burj Khalifa ("Khalifa Tower"), was built in Dubai in the United Arab Emirates, some 4,100 miles (6,598 km) west of Taipei. It was seen as a symbol of progress and modernism for Dubai, as well as for the entire Middle East. Commented Mohamed Alabbar, chair of the real estate company that developed the skyscraper, "In Burj Khalifa, we see the triumph of Dubai's vision of attaining the seemingly impossible and setting new benchmarks. The project is a declaration of the emirate's capabilities and of the resolve of its leaders and people to work hand in hand on truly awe-inspiring projects."[40]

When construction on the 163-floor Burj Khalifa was completed in 2009, the slender spire of glass and stainless steel rose 2,722 feet (830 m) above the ground, the tallest human-made structure on earth. Like Taipei 101, designers of the Burj Khalifa looked to the local culture for inspiration. Its Y-shaped plan is based on the shape of the *Hymenocallis*, a native desert flower, and the building's design incorporates elements of the local Islamic culture. Although the Burj Khalifa is located in the Middle East, designing and building it was an international undertaking. According to Alabbar, "Thousands of people from more than 100 countries have contributed to the realization of 'Burj Khalifa.' The tower embodies the spirit and optimism of global collaboration, and shows to the world what can be achieved when communities work in partnership."[41]

In 1956 renowned American architect Frank Lloyd Wright announced a plan to construct the tallest skyscraper ever conceived: a

Burj Khalifa, completed in Dubai in 2009, for several years has held the distinction of being the tallest building in the world. But that is likely to change; construction was scheduled to begin in 2013 on an even taller building in Saudi Arabia.

building 1 mile (1.6 km) in height. Many people scoffed at Wright's plan, and given construction technology of the time, the structure could never have been built. But the idea of a mile-high building did not die, it simply moved to the Middle East. By the end of the 2000s, plans were under way for Kingdom Tower, a mile-high skyscraper to be built in Saudi Arabia. Although the height of the proposed building was revised to 3,280 feet (1 km), when completed it will surpass Burj Khalifa by 558 feet (171 m)—keeping the title of the world's tallest building solidly in the Eastern Hemisphere.

Chapter THREE

A Volatile Economy

On October 29, 1929, a massive sell-off of stocks caused the US stock market to crash, driving the nation into a period of economic decline known as the Great Depression. Overnight, thousands of people lost their life savings. Hundreds of banks failed because borrowers could not afford to repay their loans. In rural America, farmers abandoned their fields as crop prices plummeted, while in the cities, jobless men resorted to selling apples on street corners to earn a few cents. Many feared that the Great Depression would never end.

It took twelve years, but on the eve of World War II, the economy finally pulled itself out of its ruinous collapse. Since then, every economic slump brings fears of a new depression. Between 1947 and 2000, America experienced eight recessions, but none as devastating as the Great Depression. Then, in the new millennium, the economy entered its worst economic period in seventy years. A combination of corporate greed, easy credit, and lax government regulations threatened to plunge the economy into a depression on a global scale.

Greed, Corruption, and Fraud

In the 1990s the Enron Corporation was one of the most powerful—and profitable—energy companies in the United States. But behind its success was a corporate culture of greed, corruption, and fraud that would ultimately destroy both the company and the lives of the executives who had made it a success.

Enron was founded as the result of a merger of two natural gas companies in 1985 by Kenneth Lay, chair of one of the merged companies. The next year Lay became chief executive officer of the newly named Enron Corporation. Enron was in the business of selling natural gas and electricity to customers worldwide. It owned the largest gas distribution system in North America, with some 36,000 miles (57,936 km) of pipelines. Enron's revenues grew in the 1990s as the company increased its market share at home and built power plants around the world. Lay and his top executives, Jeffrey Skilling and Andrew Fastow, seemed to be leading Enron toward a bright future of increased profits and satisfied stockholders. What the stockholders did not know was that they were being lied to by the very executives who promised to increase the value of their holdings.

As early as 1995 rumors of accounting irregularities circulated within Enron, but these rumors were suppressed by company executives. By 2000 Enron was the largest natural gas company in the world, with reported revenue of $100.8 billion for the year. Enron stock prices were steadily rising. But those prices were artificially inflated and did not represent the actual value of the company. In truth, Enron was billions of dollars in debt due to bad investments, accounting irregularities, and huge bonuses. To make the company appear more profitable, Enron used methods that

King of the Ponzi Scheme

Bernard Madoff was a successful investment advisor who made clients wealthy through his investment firm. What his clients did not know was that he was also making himself rich by running one of the largest scams ever perpetrated in American financial history. Madoff bilked unsuspecting investors out of some $65 billion over twenty years, until he confessed to his crimes in 2008.

Madoff used a swindle known as a Ponzi scheme, named for Charles Ponzi, an early twentieth-century con artist. In a Ponzi scheme, investors are promised very high rates of return for the money they invest. As word of the huge financial gains gets around, more people invest. The scam artist keeps huge amounts of the money for him- or herself, paying interest to early investors out of funds from later clients, rather than through legitimate investments.

Madoff provided his clients with phony positive earnings reports, which encouraged them to keep their money in his system. When the economy collapsed in 2008, his investors began asking for their original investments back. But most of the money was gone, and Madoff was exposed as a fraud. Arrested on December 11, 2008, Madoff was tried and found guilty of, among other charges, securities fraud and perjury. He was sentenced to 150 years in prison. Madoff's victims included millionaires, celebrities, and many ordinary people who lost their life savings.

were, if not illegal, at least misleading. According to author Loren Fox, "If Enron bought $100,000 worth of natural gas, then sold it an hour later for $101,000, Enron booked the full $101,000 as revenue rather than the $1,000 in gross profit it made on the deal."[42] If a company acquired by Enron began showing losses, it was shuttled into a partnership called a "special purpose entity," where its poor performance could be hidden.

Fall of an Energy Giant

The beginning of the end for Enron came in 2001. On August 14 Skilling quit the company. The next day Sherron Watkins, an Enron vice president, sent an anonymous memo to Kenneth Lay, voicing concern about the company's financial situation. The memo read, "Has Enron become a risky place to work? I am incredibly nervous that we will implode in a wave of accounting scandals. We are under too much scrutiny and there are probably one or two disgruntled 'redeployed' employees who know enough about the 'funny' accounting to get us in trouble."[43]

In October 2001 Enron reported a loss of $618 million for the previous quarter. The company's stock, which had been trading at ninety dollars per share in 2000, had plummeted to twenty dollars and continued to slide. Lay telephoned the government's top financial leaders in Washington, including the secretary of the treasury, to seek help for his failing company. But government officials declined to provide assistance. Enron had one hope left: A deal was in the works for Dynegy, a rival energy company, to purchase Enron at a bargain price. But with Enron's declining stock prices and billions of dollars in debt, the buyout fell through. It was the end for what was once one of the richest energy companies in the world. With its stock trading at sixty-one cents, Enron filed for bankruptcy on December 2, 2001.

The fallout from Enron's collapse was enormous. Nearly $11 billion of shareholder stock was wiped out. Enron employees who had company stock as part or all of their retirement plans were hit-hard after the collapse. Charles Prestwood, a retired employee, lamented, "I had all my savings, everything in Enron stock. I lost $1.3 million."[44] Fastow pleaded guilty to conspiracy charges and was sentenced to ten years in prison. Lay and Skilling were tried and convicted on numerous counts of fraud and conspiracy. Skilling was sentenced to twenty-four years in prison; Lay died of a heart attack before he could be sentenced. The Enron scandal was just the first incident in what would become a decade of economic upheaval.

The Housing Bubble

When fifty-three-year-old Donna Marie Pearce asked her mortgage broker about refinancing the condominium she had recently purchased, she received a shocking answer. Although the Connecticut nanny had been told that she could refinance to lower her interest rate, she now learned that a fee of several thousand dollars would be required. Even if she could afford the fee, after just six months of paying on the mortgage, Pearce did not have enough equity in the property to be able to secure a new loan. Falling behind on payments she could no longer afford, Pearce was on the brink of losing her home. "It shakes up your whole life," she recalled. "You think you're getting somewhere, and it just pulls the rug out from under you."[45]

Pearce was just one innocent victim of a real estate contract called a subprime loan. And if these types of mortgages were disconcerting to individual homeowners, the effect they had on the nation's—and the world's—economy was devastating.

"I do believe in the American Dream. Owning a home is a part of that dream, it just is. Right here in America if you own your own home, you're realizing the American Dream."[46] When George W. Bush made that statement in June 2002, the American housing market was booming. In 1995 the median price for a single-family home was $133,900; in 2002 it had reached $187,600—a 40 percent increase. People wanted to be a part of the American Dream, and lending institutions were eager to help them realize that dream. To take advantage of this "housing bubble," banks began to relax their criteria for issuing mortgages. At the time, would-be homeowners had to show lenders they were financially able to own a home. Lenders checked a potential customer's employment history, salary, savings, and other financial information. When approved, borrowers paid a down payment and were issued a standard mortgage, usually lasting thirty years at a fixed interest rate.

Risky Mortgages

Many people who wanted to buy a house could not meet the requirements for a standard mortgage. The reasons ranged from not making enough money or being unemployed to having a poor credit history. Not wanting to turn a potential customer away, mortgage lenders got creative. They began to issue mortgages without checking employment status or credit history. Many of these new mortgages required no down

The 2000s saw the collapse of the US housing market. As home values plummeted, many homeowners defaulted on their loan payments, which in turn led to a record number of home foreclosures during the period known as the Great Recession.

payment or had attractively low initial interest rates that would increase over time (although not all borrowers understood this). These loans were called subprime mortgages because they were issued to people who could not afford a standard loan. Subprime mortgages were risky for the lenders, because the threat of borrowers defaulting on the loans was greater than that of standard mortgage holders. Nevertheless, the housing bubble kept growing, and banks kept lending to almost anyone who wanted a mortgage. The value of subprime mortgages grew from $160 billion in 2001 to $540 billion in 2004. But just like a soap bubble, the housing bubble eventually had to burst.

In 2006 home prices had hit their peak and were starting to fall. People with subprime mortgages who could no longer afford their monthly payments had little choice but to default on their loans. By the end of 2006, nearly 1 million homeowners had experienced loan defaults. Banks foreclosed on homes when the owners defaulted, then tried to sell the homes at bargain prices. With so many houses going back on the market, prices plunged even further. By the end of 2008, more than 3 million foreclosures were recorded. According to the Federal Reserve, the total loss of wealth caused by the bubble bursting was a staggering $7.38 trillion. The average homeowner lost 55 percent of the value of his or her home. The damage was more than just monetary: countless jobs in the construction, real estate, and banking industries were lost as well. But the worst fallout from the housing bubble was yet to come. And when it did, it would have global consequences.

The Great Recession

The US economy was thriving in the early 2000s. Unemployment was down, investing was up, and people were buying everything from houses to cars to the latest electronic gadgets. One of the main reasons for this growing economy was the booming real estate market. According to journalist Justin Fox, "To a remarkable extent, housing drove the entire economy. Real estate, residential construction and three other housing-related Labor Department categories together add up to 6.6% of U.S. employment. But they accounted for 46% of the new jobs created in the U.S. between January 2001 and May 2006."[47]

Local banks were taking in record amounts of money from the mortgages sold during the housing boom. Looking for more ways to invest this money, they turned their attention to investment banks. An investment bank is different from a local bank in that it does not take deposits or issue loans. Instead, investment banks act as intermediaries to help individuals and companies invest their assets. One way they do this is to issue securities backed by financial assets such as stocks or bonds—or mortgages. Local banks began selling their home loans to investment banks. The investment banks packaged these mortgages into bundles called mortgage-backed securities (MBSs), which they then sold to private and corporate investors. Billions of dollars of these securities were sold in the early to mid-2000s. At first, it was a winning situation for everyone: The lending banks made money, the investment banks made money, and so did the purchasers of the MBSs. Investors were sure their money was safe. After all, real estate was a solid investment. But inside these bundles lurked a financial time bomb: the subprime mortgages.

Most subprime mortgages started at a low interest rate, but after a few years the rate jumped. Borrowers who could not afford the increase lost their homes. As foreclosed homes were put back on the market, prices tumbled, and so did the investment banks' income. Federal Reserve chair Ben Bernanke acknowledged the growing crisis. "The recent expansion of the subprime market," he said, "was clearly accompanied by deterioration in underwriting standards and in some cases, by abusive lending practices and outright fraud."[48] As America's central banking system, the Federal Reserve began investigating the subprime mortgage industry to determine if stricter regulation was necessary. Bernanke also noted that things "likely will get worse before they get better."[49] No one knew just how much worse things would get.

The news came as a shock to the US financial community: Bear Stearns, one of the nation's largest investment banks, was in financial collapse. Too many losses on bad MBSs had left Bear Stearns with little operating cash. To avoid bankruptcy, the bank was bought out at a bargain price by another large bank, JPMorgan Chase. Many other investment firms were also facing collapse. One of them was Merrill Lynch, an investment company in business since 1914. On September, 14, 2008, Merrill Lynch was sold to the Bank of America. The next day the investment firm Lehman Brothers declared bankruptcy, with outstanding debts of more than $600 billion. It was the largest bankruptcy in US history to that time.

Global Fallout

As the Great Recession was blasting through the American economy, the fallout was being felt throughout the world. Fears of bank runs, where depositors rush to withdraw money from banks they are afraid will fail, were growing. "In this day and age, a bank run spreads around the world, not around the block,"[50] observed economist Thomas Mayer of the Deutsche Bank in Germany. Many foreign banks had invested in American MBSs, and they recorded major losses when the value of the MBSs tumbled. The United Kingdom, France, Germany, and Italy all suffered their worst economic performance in decades. In Japan and China investors began selling off their holdings in US mortgages as their value declined.

With the recession growing to global proportions, the United States began taking steps to deal with the crisis. Just days after the Lehman

A Global Recession

The United States was not the only country touched by the Great Recession. From Europe to Asia, the financial crisis quickly spread to become a global problem affecting millions. In Europe unemployment rose, housing prices fell, and investors suffered massive losses. In Germany industrial output decreased at the fastest rate in a decade. Spain's housing crisis prompted the finance minister to declare that the nation was headed toward its deepest recession in fifty years. Japan and China both felt the impact of the recession as well.

The nation of Iceland was especially hard-hit by the recession. In 2008 Iceland's stock market lost 90 percent of its value, and the country's inflation rate jumped to 18 percent. The value of the krona, Iceland's currency, plunged 80 percent, and its three major banks collapsed. The Icelandic government's response to the financial crisis was different than that of the US government. Instead of bailing out the banks, Iceland aided its citizens by helping reduce homeowners' debt and providing subsidies to lower mortgage interest rates. Although the nation had to take some $10 billion in loans from the International Monetary Fund, it repaid the debt ahead of schedule.

Iceland's president, Olafur Ragnar Grimmson, explained his nation's remarkable recovery. "We were wise enough not to follow the traditional prevailing orthodoxies of the Western financial world in the last 30 years. We introduced currency controls, we let the banks fail, we provided support for the poor, and we didn't introduce austerity measures like you're seeing in Europe."

Quoted in Tracy Greenstein, "Iceland's Stabilized Economy Is a Surprising Success Story," *Forbes*, February 20, 2013. www .forbes.com.

Brothers bankruptcy, Secretary of the Treasury Henry Paulson proposed a plan to rescue banks burdened with subprime mortgages. Under this plan, the government would buy $700 billion worth of MBSs from struggling investment banks. Presenting the proposal to the American people in a televised address on September 24, 2008, Bush said:

> We're in the midst of a serious financial crisis, and the federal government is responding with decisive action. . . . There has been a widespread loss of confidence, and major sectors of America's financial system are at risk of shutting down. . . . In the short term, this will free up banks to resume the flow of credit to American families and businesses, and this will help our economy grow.[51]

Bush signed the bailout plan, officially called the Emergency Economic Stabilization Act, into law on October 3. This new law created the Troubled Assets Relief Program (TARP) to allocate the $700 billion fund. Although the initial $700 billion was reduced to $470 billion, hundreds of banks and financial institutions received TARP funds. General Motors and Chrysler, two of the "big three" Detroit automakers, also received billions in bailout cash to stave off bankruptcy. TARP, along with other government programs, returned a measure of stability to the US economy. By mid-2009 unemployment was easing and the gross domestic product, which is an indication of the health of an economy, began to rise. Officially, the Great Recession ended in June 2009. But the economic rebound has been sluggish. By 2011 jobs were still difficult to find, and median household income actually declined. Some economists say that the recovery has been the slowest since the Great Depression.

Globalizing Economies

It is a familiar scene: customers lining up at their local McDonald's restaurant for a quick snack or a family meal. But what they order may be anything but familiar. Ebi Filet-O, Croque McDo, and Bubur Ayam McD are just a few examples of the exotic (at least to Americans) fare available in McDonald's restaurants around the world. Dining under the Golden Arches is now an international affair and an example of how globalization has changed the face of business in the twenty-first century.

Globalization, the increased interconnectivity of nations, is a relatively new term, but the international commerce to which it refers is not. The Silk Road, an ancient trade route that originated in China in the second century BCE and spread as far as Egypt and Rome, was active for at least sixteen hundred years. Before World War I international trade grew rapidly, thanks to the development of railroads, steamships, and the telegraph. By the 2000s the increasing importance of the computer and the Internet helped spur further advances in globalization. "A powerful force drives the world toward a converging commonality," wrote Harvard professor Theodore Levitt, "and that force is technology. It has made isolated places and impoverished peoples eager for modernity's allurements. Almost everyone everywhere wants all the things they have heard about, seen, or experienced via the new technologies."[52]

The Newly Industrialized Countries

But it was not just technology that enabled this boom in worldwide commerce, which in 2005 reached $8 trillion. Many nations were changing the way they viewed their own economies and the role they wanted to play in the global marketplace. Called newly industrialized countries, these nations exhibited growth in manufacturing along with a rapidly expanding economy increasingly built on exports. Countries having an agricultural-based economy began producing more manufactured goods. Many countries became more open to foreign investment, which brought an influx of capital into their economies. Nations considered newly industrialized countries include Mexico, the Philippines, Brazil, India, Turkey, and most importantly, China.

Enacting political reforms in the People's Republic of China, 1970s and 1980s Communist Party leader Deng Xiaoping led the nation toward a market economy, where production of goods is based on the supply and demand of the marketplace. Many of the state-owned enterprises, industries run by the Chinese government, became privately run companies. "The major reform achievement has been in privatizing state enterprises," commented Chinese economist Fan Gang. "The private sector accounts for 70% of gross domestic product."[53] China's economic growth exploded, rising some 9.5 percent per year. It is predicted that China's economy will become the largest in the world, surpassing that of the United States, sometime before the middle of the twenty-first century.

China is perhaps the premier example of how globalization can improve the lives of a nation's citizens. Proponents of globalization say that it brings a higher standard of living to underdeveloped countries. The middle class expands as more people can afford more and better consumer products. "My parents were both teachers when they were my age," a young Chinese worker said in 2007, "and they earned 30 yuan ($3.70) a month. I earn 4,000 yuan ($500) a month, live comfortably and feel I have better opportunities than my parents did."[54]

Evidence of China's growing economy can be seen on a busy street in Shanghai (pictured). The 2000s brought higher wages and an improved standard of living for many Chinese workers.

Globalization has its critics as well as its champions. In November 2009 three thousand people protested a meeting of the World Trade Organization (WTO) in Geneva, Switzerland. As an organization promoting globalization, the WTO was a symbol for the real or imagined injustices of the trend. Protesters were afraid that globalization meant spreading a Western, capitalist worldview at the expense of the workers and cultures of developing nations. Many felt that globalization was a threat to the environment, since huge, multinational corporations must eventually acquire more and more natural resources. Some even feared that democracy would suffer and predicted that global corporations would attain more political power than governments.

The economic world weathered many challenges in the first decade of the twenty-first century. But more challenges lay ahead, this time in the world of politics.

Chapter FOUR

Government and Politics

In the United States the 2000s began with the Supreme Court deciding the outcome of a presidential election and ended with the first African American chief executive taking the oath of office. In between, the world was rocked by terrorism and ravaged by war; it witnessed a renewed sense of US patriotism, the fall of a hated dictator, and the resurgence of piracy on the high seas.

George W. Bush, in his inaugural address on January 20, 2001, spoke optimistically about the role of the United States in the new decade: "We will build our defenses beyond challenge, lest weakness invite challenge. We will confront weapons of mass destruction, so that a new century is spared new horrors. The enemies of liberty and our country should make no mistake: America remains engaged in the world, by history and by choice, shaping a balance of power that favors freedom."[55]

As the sole remaining superpower, America could not avoid being engaged in the world. It was a world that presented challenges as well as opportunities not only to the United States but to civilized nations everywhere.

Terrorists Attack the United States

On September 11, 2001, radical Islamists supported by terrorist organization al Qaeda flew commercial airliners into the World Trade Center in New York; the Pentagon outside Washington, DC; and a field in Pennsylvania. These acts of violence, which killed nearly three thousand people, set the tone for Bush's presidency and for other parts of the world during the 2000s. On September 20, 2001, exactly eight months after his inaugural address, the president spoke to a joint session of Congress. The speech, televised throughout the world, announced that the United States was embarking on a different kind of war:

> Our war on terror begins with al-Qaeda, but it does not end there. It will not end until every terrorist group of global reach has been found, stopped and defeated. . . . We will direct every resource at our command—every means of diplomacy, every tool of intelligence, every instrument of law enforcement, every financial influence, and every necessary weapon of war—to the disruption and to the defeat of the global terror network.[56]

Although only the United States was attacked on 9/11, other countries, including Great Britain, Norway, Turkey, Japan, Australia, and South Korea, supported the United States in its War on Terror. On September 28 the United Nations Security Council called on member nations to "work together urgently to prevent and suppress terrorist acts."[57] The first priority of the war was to find and bring to justice the al Qaeda leaders who planned and financed the attacks. Most of them were suspected of hiding in Afghanistan, protected by that nation's fundamentalist Islamic government, the Taliban. Operation Enduring Freedom, a military operation launched by the United States and a coalition of other nations, began with air strikes against Taliban targets in Afghanistan on October 7, 2001. After several months of air strikes and ground combat, the Taliban was removed from power, and terrorist training camps run by al Qaeda were shut down. But many Taliban and al Qaeda leaders fled to Pakistan, Afghanistan's neighbor. Among these fugitives was Osama bin Laden, the founder of al Qaeda.

Vulnerabilities

September 11 was not the first time Bin Laden's organization, or groups affiliated with it, committed acts of terrorism. In October 2000 al Qaeda–trained operatives detonated a small boat filled with explosives next to the USS *Cole*, a navy destroyer anchored at Aden harbor in the nation of Yemen. Seventeen sailors were killed and thirty-nine injured. Throughout the decade terrorists mounted deadly attacks worldwide, targeting innocent civilians who were going about their everyday activities. No country was immune from terrorism. Indonesia, Turkey, Spain, the United Kingdom, and Algeria all experienced terrorist attacks, often accomplished by suicide bombers who willingly became martyrs for their cause. The death toll mounted: 202 fatalities in Bali in 2002; 191 killed in Madrid in 2004; 52 killed in London in 2005. Other terrorist plots were foiled. A man with explosives in his shoe unsuccessfully tried to destroy an airliner in 2001. A plot to destroy the New York Stock Exchange was thwarted in 2004.

The Taliban's expulsion from Afghanistan did not last long. In 2002 groups of Taliban insurgents began fighting against the forces of the International Security Assistance Force, which had been established by the United Nations to help Afghanistan create a secure environment and reconstruct a stable government. Insurgent attacks sharply increased in

President George W. Bush greets US troops in Iraq in November 2003. In March of that year a coalition force led by the United States invaded Iraq.

2006, with more than one thousand civilian injuries or deaths recorded during the year. Suicide bombings, once a rarity in Afghanistan, increased 600 percent that same year.

Years after the 9/11 attacks, it was unclear if the global War on Terror would, or even could, be ended. In 2002 Bush declared, "The characteristics we most cherish—our freedom, our cities, our systems of movement, and modern life—are vulnerable to terrorism. This vulnerability will persist long after we bring to justice those responsible for the September 11 attacks."[58] In 2008 America elected a new president, Barack Obama. In 2011 Bin Laden was killed in a raid by US Navy SEALs. And around the world, the Global War on Terrorism continued.

Taking Preemptive Action

When the Global War on Terrorism began, US military policy was based on decades of tension between the United States and the Soviet Union; this was known as the Cold War. After World War II the Soviet Union had installed Communist governments in Poland, Czechoslovakia, and other eastern European nations. To counter this spread of communism, the United States employed a strategy called containment, restricting communism to those nations already in the Soviet bloc.

Soviet-style communism ended in 1991, and by 2002 Bush saw a need for a new strategy for the War on Terror. "New threats require new thinking," Bush told graduates of the US Military Academy on June 1. "Containment is not possible when unbalanced dictators with weapons of mass destruction can deliver those weapons on missiles or secretly provide them to terrorist allies."[59] *The National Security Strategy of the United States of America*, published in September 2002, explained: "To forestall or prevent such hostile acts by our adversaries, the United States will, if necessary, act preemptively in exercising our inherent right of self-defense."[60] This concept, known as the Bush Doctrine, said that the United States had the right to strike first at any suspected threat, even before being attacked. In 2003, while the debate over the legality of the plan continued, the Bush Doctrine was put into action.

The US Invasion of Iraq

The first area of engagement was Iraq. The Bush administration saw Iraq as a threat to world peace and as a nation whose dictatorial regime needed to be overthrown. Its president, Saddam Hussein, governed his country as a brutal dictatorship. He had used chemical weapons against the Kurdish population living in northern Iraq in the 1980s, and members of the Bush administration feared that these or other weapons of mass destruction (WMDs) such as nuclear or biological weapons might ultimately be used against the United States or its allies. Officials in the Bush administration also suggested that Saddam had ties to al Qaeda.

United Nations inspectors went to Iraq to determine if Saddam had WMDs, but they got little cooperation from the Iraqi government. After several unsuccessful attempts by UN inspectors to verify the presence of WMDs, the Bush administration concluded that Iraq was hiding its WMDs and that the danger could no longer be ignored. On March 19, 2003, under the name Operation Iraqi Freedom, a coalition force led by the United States attacked Iraq. As US cruise missiles and stealth bombers pounded Baghdad, Iraq's capital, Bush addressed the nation on television. "My fellow citizens, at this hour, American and coalition forces are in the early stages of military operations to disarm Iraq, to free its people and to defend the world from grave danger."[61] Coalition ground forces launched their assault from Kuwait, just south of Iraq. Baghdad fell on April 9, but by then Saddam had fled.

For nearly nine months Saddam remained at large amid rumors and false sightings. Then on December 14, 2003, US infantry troops discovered Saddam hiding in a concealed underground bunker on a farm not far from his hometown of Tikrit. This so-called spider hole was near a dilapidated two-room hut where Saddam apparently lived; he moved to the bunker whenever US troops seemed close. A far cry from the sumptuous palaces that were his former residences, the hut was dirty and strewn with rubbish and rotting food. A trench outside served as the bathroom.

Pulled to the surface and arrested, Saddam looked nothing like the powerful dictator he once had been. He was disheveled and dirty with a scruffy gray beard, and he appeared disoriented and surprised that he had been captured. "I am Saddam Hussein," he reportedly said, "the duly

WMDs Justified the Iraq War

Through numerous resolutions issued between 1990 and 2002, the United Nations ordered Iraqi dictator Saddam Hussein to destroy all WMDs in his possession. When UN inspectors tried on several occasions to verify his compliance, Saddam obstructed their efforts. George W. Bush and his advisors interpreted Saddam's actions as confirmation that he was hiding WMDs and cited this as justification for the US invasion of Iraq. In a televised March 2003 address to the nation, Bush stated:

> Intelligence gathered by this and other governments leaves no doubt that the Iraq regime continues to possess and conceal some of the most lethal weapons ever devised. This regime has already used weapons of mass destruction against Iraq's neighbors and against Iraq's people. The regime has a history of reckless aggression in the Middle East. It has a deep hatred of America and our friends. And it has aided, trained and harbored terrorists, including operatives of al Qaeda.
>
> The danger is clear: using chemical, biological or, one day, nuclear weapons, obtained with the help of Iraq, the terrorists could fulfill their stated ambitions and kill thousands or hundreds of thousands of innocent people in our country, or any other. The United States and other nations did nothing to deserve or invite this threat. But we will do everything to defeat it. Instead of drifting along toward tragedy, we will set a course toward safety. Before the day of horror can come, before it is too late to act, this danger will be removed.

George W. Bush, "Address to the Nation," White House, March 17, 2003. http://georgewbush-whitehouse.archives.gov.

elected president of Iraq. I am willing to negotiate." To that, one of the soldiers replied, "Well, President Bush sends his regards."[62] Saddam was tried for war crimes and crimes against humanity by the Iraqi Special Tribunal. On November 5, 2006, he was convicted and sentenced to death by hanging. The sentence was carried out on December 6.

An Illegal War

The Iraq War, which officially ended in December 2011, amassed a toll of nearly forty-five hundred US soldiers killed, more than one hundred thousand Iraqi civilians dead, and an expenditure of almost $1.7 trillion. But the legacy of this conflict is more than numbers: The war changed the world's view of the United States. Although several countries had

PERSPECTIVES

The Iraq War Was Not Justified

Hans Blix was the executive chair of the United Nations Monitoring, Verification and Inspection Commission (UNMOVIC) from March 2000 to June 2003. UNMOVIC was created to monitor Iraq's compliance with United Nations resolutions for disarming its WMD capabilities. What Blix and his team found, or more accurately did not find, in Iraq contradicted the impression given by George W. Bush of a dangerous nation filled with WMDs. According to Blix:

> President Bush has said that war and armed force is only the means of last resort; it was not the means of last resort in March last year. On the contrary, one could say that the evidence was beginning to fall apart. There was the tendency, which I commented upon in the Security Council, of equating "unaccounted for" weapons with "existing" ones. Then, as of January 2003, when the United States and others gave us sites to visit, in no case did we find any weapons of mass destruction. And they claimed they were the best sites. I said publicly, if these were the best sites, what were the rest? . . .
>
> Here a whole war was started on intelligence that they firmly believed in, and it is shaky. I understand that no other grounds would have been enough to persuade Congress or the U.K. Parliament on this one. If they had said, "We want to create a democracy"—well, I don't think the Congress would have said, "We'll go to war in Iraq to create a democracy."

Quoted in *National Journal*, "Blix: Iraq War Was Not Justified," National Journal Group, March 31, 2004. www3.national journal.com.

supported and assisted US military efforts in Iraq, the United Nations Security Council, which had not sanctioned the war, considered it to be unlawful. "I have indicated it was not in conformity with the UN charter," UN Secretary General Kofi Annan said in 2004. "From our point of view and from the charter point of view it was illegal."[63]

No WMDs, the primary reason stated for the war, were found in Iraq. Nor was any link between Saddam and al Qaeda discovered. Polls as recent as 2012 reveal that people in many nations think less favorably of the United States as a result of the War on Terror. The United States incurred many losses during the Iraq War, including the lives of courageous military men and women. But the loss of international goodwill may have long-lasting ramifications for US interests.

Pirates of Somalia

Richard Phillips, captain of the cargo ship *Maersk Alabama*, entered the ship's bridge on the morning of April 8, 2009. He was attending to routine duties when a sailor interrupted him. "Boat approaching," the mate said, "three point one miles out, astern."[64] Just a few days before, some small, powered skiffs had buzzed the ship, but high waves drove them back. With calm seas on this particular morning, Phillips knew that he would not be so lucky again. He quickly sounded the alarm to let his crew know that Somali pirates were headed directly for the *Alabama*.

The eastern African nation of Somalia had been in chaos since the beginning of a civil war in 1991. As a result of the hostilities, the people of Somalia suffered a famine that killed three hundred thousand people. Thousands more fled the country while others died in the fighting. Livelihoods were lost, including those of Somali fishermen whose earnings were destroyed by illegal fishing off the coast of Somalia. With no government to protect their waters, many fishermen took to piracy. "When we tried to fish, we didn't get anything," said one pirate. "We became very angry. Everyone was coming. Where can we get our fish? So we decided to attack the [illegal fishermen]."[65] Lack of government oversight also lured international corporations to Somali waters for the dumping of toxic waste. This further decimated the fish population, giving the pirates a new, more lucrative, target for their attacks.

Ransom Demands

These modern pirates are a far cry from the buccaneers depicted in popular literature. Armed with automatic weapons and rocket-propelled grenades, Somali pirates approached their targets in swift, small motorboats launched from a larger ship. Small groups of young pirates boarded the target vessel, demanding a ransom for the release of the ship and its crew. Often, paying the ransom was seen as a good business decision. "From a purely economic point of view," said J. Peter Pham, associate professor of justice studies, political science, and Africana studies at James Madison University in Harrisonburg, Virginia, "it makes a great deal of sense if you have a cargo ship that is worth at least $20 to $30 million, it stands to reason that paying them a million dollars to get it back is an economically rational decision."[66]

Swift capitulation to the pirates' demands may have encouraged even more piracy. Ransoms increased from an average of $150,000 in 2005 to $5.4 million in 2010. But ransoms are not the only expenses incurred. Higher insurance rates, protective equipment for ships, legal fees for prosecuting pirates, and rerouting ships away from dangerous sea lanes all add to the costs of piracy. One estimate places the annual cost of piracy to the shipping industry as high as $6.9 billion. Many of these costs are ultimately passed on to the consumer, resulting in higher prices at the supermarket and department store.

In November 2008 piracy was thrust into the forefront of world news when Somali pirates hijacked the supertanker *Sirius Star*. The pirates sailed the vessel to a port in Somalia and demanded $25 million in ransom for the return of the ship and its $100 million cargo of oil. Held for nearly two months, the tanker was released after its owners paid the pirates $3 million. The incident showed that even huge ships were vulnerable to pirate attacks. That year a total of forty ships were hijacked, and ransoms of between $500,000 and $2 million were paid. By the late 2000s international cooperation and increased naval patrols made it more difficult for the Somali pirates to succeed in their illegal trade. Many pirates have been captured and tried for piracy and, in some cases, murder.

The capture of the *Maersk Alabama* had a successful ending—but not for the four pirates who hijacked the vessel. Phillips was taken hostage and held for five days in a lifeboat while the pirates negotiated. On

April 12, 2009, in a display of pinpoint marksmanship, US Navy SEAL snipers killed three of the pirates on the lifeboat and rescued Phillips unharmed. The fourth pirate, who had been subdued by the *Alabama's* crew, was brought to trial and ultimately sentenced to thirty-three years in prison.

Pham argues that piracy is terrorism and a crime against humanity. "For centuries, international law actually described pirates as . . . enemies of the human race because they, in essence, rebelled against the international system and peaceful commerce," says Pham. "And certainly in the age in which we live today, the disruptive effect of even the small number of successful pirate hijackings is staggering."[67]

A President in the Making

The Fleet Center in Boston, Massachusetts, was packed for the Democratic National Convention on July 27, 2004. While presidential candidate John Kerry and his running mate John Edwards were the focal point of the convention, the young African American state senator who gave the keynote address that night captivated the crowd. His speech drew cheers from the crowd and rave reviews from the political pundits. Pennsylvania delegate Marsha DeFazio said, "I think he could be our first black president."[68] Her prediction came true four years later when Barack Obama was elected the forty-fourth president of the United States.

Born in Hawaii, the son of a Kenyan father and white mother, Obama grew up in Hawaii and Indonesia. After graduating from Columbia University, he worked as a community organizer in Chicago, helping to improve conditions for African Americans. He then attended Harvard Law School, after which he worked as a civil rights attorney and taught constitutional law at the University of Chicago. A career in politics was never far from his mind as a way to help people. In November 1996 Obama was elected Illinois state senator from the Thirteenth District, representing a large part of Chicago's predominantly African American South Side. His ever-present desire to help even more people led him to seek national political office.

In 1999 Bobby Rush, an Illinois member of the US House of Representatives, was up for reelection. Against the counsel of friends and advisers, Obama challenged him in the Democratic primary. Rush was a veteran politician and four-term representative with both experience and name recognition. Obama's campaign stumbled when he missed an important Illinois Senate vote on gun control. He realized that his campaign was in trouble. "Less than halfway into the campaign, I knew in my bones that I was going to lose,"[69] he says. When the votes were tallied

Americans elected the nation's first African American president in 2008. Democrat Barack Obama defeated Republican John McCain by nearly 10 million votes.

on March 21, 2000, Rush had trounced Obama by a margin of two to one. It was the only loss in Obama's political career.

One lesson that Obama learned from the failed campaign was that he had to overcome his Eastern-elite, Harvard image in order to cultivate African American voters. "I can't just show up being black and think I'm going to get the black vote," he said. "I have to reach out and communicate my track record—who I am and what I care about."[70] He also learned that he was adept at raising money for his campaigns. These lessons helped him in his next campaign. In November 2004 Obama was elected US senator from Illinois, garnering 70 percent of the vote against his Republican opponent. As a junior US senator, Obama worked hard for his Illinois constituents. But there was one more challenge ahead: a run for the White House.

The Presidential Campaign

On the frigid morning of February 10, 2007, Obama spoke to a crowd of some fifteen thousand in Springfield, Illinois. "In the shadow of the Old State Capitol," he said, "where Lincoln once called on a divided house to stand together, where common hopes and common dreams still live, I stand before you today to announce my candidacy for President of the United States."[71]

Obama had serious competition for his party's nomination. New York senator Hillary Rodham Clinton, wife of former president Bill Clinton, was favored to win the nomination. As the primary elections approached, Obama's fund-raising skills went into high gear. Using the Internet, Obama raised huge amounts of money, mostly from small donors rather than from large corporations. In January 2008 alone, Obama raised a record $32 million.

Obama's campaign was not without controversy. Some people questioned his eligibility for the presidency, claiming he was not born in the United States. Others believed he was secretly a Muslim who would play into the hands of America's terrorist adversaries. His personal acquaintances also came under scrutiny. Obama's association with a 1960s radical named William Ayers was questioned, as was his membership in a church pastored by Jeremiah Wright, whose sermons were harshly critical of the United States and white Americans. Obama severed his ties with Wright's church, and the other allegations were all proved to be unfounded.

But no amount of controversy could stop the momentum that Obama had gained. By June Clinton had dropped out of the race and endorsed Obama as the Democratic candidate. His running mate was Joe Biden, a senior senator who had served for twenty-six years. Their Republican opponents were Arizona senator John McCain and Alaska governor Sarah Palin. Obama ran a campaign based on the ideas of hope and change—that the United States needed a change from old-style politics to the new vision of a younger generation. Obama represented that new generation: he was forty-seven years old, while political veteran McCain had recently celebrated his seventy-second birthday. At campaign rallies, Obama supporters' chants of "Yes, we can!" acknowledged their hope for the future.

America's First African American President

Obama's poll numbers had steadily increased throughout the summer, and by election eve he was 7.3 points ahead of McCain. Early on the morning of November 4, Obama and his wife, Michelle, cast their votes. Throughout the day millions of Americans did likewise. By the time the polls closed across the country that evening, Obama had been elected the first African American president of the United States, defeating McCain by nearly 10 million votes.

On the steps of the US Capitol on January 20, 2009, Obama took the oath of office. In his inaugural address he acknowledged the ordeals of war and economic hardship facing the nation. "Today I say to you that the challenges we face are real. They are serious and they are many. They will not be met easily or in a short span of time. But know this America: They will be met."[72]

Chapter FIVE

Exploring New Frontiers

The turn of a century is not only a symbolic celebration of change, it can signal a break between old and new. Before the nineteenth century gave way to the twentieth, life was slow-paced. Visiting a friend often meant traveling over miles of rutted or muddy roads in a horse and buggy. People entertained themselves by making their own music, playing parlor games, or simply chatting face-to-face. But even as the year 1900 approached, change was literally in the air. Two Ohio bicycle makers, Wilbur and Orville Wright were already experimenting with flight. Early automobiles chugged noisily down the streets, and entertainment was being transformed from home-grown to mass-produced as Thomas Edison's phonograph and kinetoscope (movie viewer) gained popularity. The Wright brothers, Edison, and many other forward-thinking individuals were creating a technological transformation the likes of which had never before been seen.

As the twenty-first century dawned, a similarly momentous transformation was taking place in both science and technology. Among the many noteworthy events were the mapping of the human genome, the arrival on Mars of two mobile robots assigned the task of exploring the planet, and the introduction of electronic devices that would keep people connected and entertained twenty-four hours a day.

The iRevolution

In December 1877 Edison made the world's first sound recording, a recitation of "Mary Had a Little Lamb," pressed into a tin foil–covered cylinder on his newly invented phonograph. Since that time, most recordings have been made in analog format, the process Edison used. Whether it was indentations in tin foil, grooves in a vinyl disc, or magnetic particles on a tape, the sound was recorded as an "analog," or exact copy, of the original. When digital audio technology was developed in the late twentieth century, things began to change.

In digital recording, analog sounds are converted into binary language, the ones and zeroes that computers can read. Digital audio files can be downloaded from the Internet and stored on computer hard drives. As the popularity of downloading music exploded, people became used to listening to their favorite songs on their computers. But they also wanted to take their music with them wherever they went. Most portable music players, like the Sony Walkman, played analog tape cassettes. But the digital world called for something revolutionary. Through his company, Apple Inc., Steve Jobs brought about that revolution.

By 2000 there were already portable digital music players on the market, but their complicated software made them difficult to use. Apple solved this problem by developing iTunes, a simple but powerful music program for Macintosh computers. Then Jobs tapped Jon Rubenstein, an Apple engineer, to create the player. "I don't know whose idea it was to do a music player," Rubenstein said, "but Steve jumped on it pretty quick and he asked me to look into it."[73] Rubenstein began gathering components for the player, including a battery, an LCD screen, and a tiny hard drive. "I went back to Steve and said, 'I know how to do this. I've got all the parts.' He said, 'Go for it.'"[74]

In early 2001 Rubenstein and his team at Apple went to work. They showed prototypes to Jobs, who would approve or reject every aspect of the player. Jobs was obsessed with elegant design and simplicity of function. For example, he insisted that songs be accessible in no more than three clicks of the player's trackwheel. On October 23, 2001, the player, now named iPod, was unveiled. Jobs said, "This amazing little device holds a thousand songs, and it goes right in my pocket."[75] No other player came close to the iPod's massive storage or long-lasting battery. About 125,000 iPods were sold in the first few months after its release. New models, such as the iPod Nano, iPod Shuffle, and iPod Touch, were developed in the next few years. By the end of the decade, more than 300 million iPods had been sold.

Technology journalist Jared T. Miller wrote in *Time* magazine that the iPod "completely redefined the experience of listening to music, as well as making it."[76] Its iconic white earbuds were seen everywhere as people tuned out the world and tuned in to their own musical soundtrack. Sales of cassettes and CDs plummeted, and radio stations no longer controlled what people listened to. But Jobs was not finished innovating, and next he set his sights on the cell phone.

Apple CEO Steve Jobs shows off the company's new iPod MP3 player in 2001. Consumers jumped on the new device, reveling in its huge storage capacity, long-lasting battery, and easy operation.

Reading 2.0

When Johannes Gutenberg invented the movable-type printing press around 1450, it revolutionized the way books were printed, distributed, and read. Five hundred fifty years later, another publishing revolution took place, sending shock waves through the well-established publishing industry.

Electronic books, or e-books, downloaded to devices called e-readers, have become a popular alternative to paper-and-ink books. Several e-readers were marketed in the early 2000s, but it was not until Amazon released its Kindle in 2007 that the popularity of e-books began to soar. E-readers have several advantages over their paper counterparts. They can hold thousands of books in a convenient, portable format, without destroying a single tree. New content can be downloaded from the Internet in seconds, and integrated dictionaries and note-taking functions add increased usefulness.

The popularity of e-books has been growing. In 2011 Amazon sold more e-books than print books. By 2012 e-books outsold hardcover books for the first time over the entire publishing industry. As sales of lower-priced e-books began to take a bite out of print book sales, publishing profits fell. Book publishers and readers can expect more changes ahead.

The Birth of the iPhone

The birth of the iPhone was, in many ways, like the origin of the iPod. Many cell phones were on the market, but to Jobs they were complicated and their designs were not elegant. Jobs knew Apple could do better, so in 2005 the company began by trying to rework its iPod to make it into a phone. Dialing a number with the iPod's trackwheel proved awkward, so a touch-sensitive glass screen was developed instead. This had the potential to make the iPhone more versatile than phones with physical keyboards. "Think of all the innovations we'd be able to adapt," Jobs said, "if we did the keyboard onscreen with software."[77] As always, style was crucial, and the iPhone became an object of beauty with its glass screen and stainless steel back.

When Jobs publicly introduced the iPhone in January 2007, he said, "Every once in a while a revolutionary product comes along that changes everything."[78] The iPhone did just that, combining an iPod, a cell phone, and Internet connectivity in one elegant device. When the iPhone finally went on sale in June, people lined up outside Apple stores to make sure they got one. It was the beginning of the "smart phone" revolution that kept people connected to the Internet and to each other wherever they went.

Cracking the Genome

Whether a person has blond or black hair, is tall or short, or has brown or blue eyes is determined by the genes inherited from his or her parents. Genes reside on chromosomes, which are made up of deoxyribonucleic acid (DNA), and pass along the genetic instructions from one generation to the next. Along with determining physical appearance, genes also play a role in a person's health. The absence or mutation of just one gene can make someone susceptible to a deadly disease such as cystic fibrosis or Huntington's disease. Learning more about how

---

Stem Cells

Actor Michael J. Fox starred in such hits as TV's *Family Ties* and the *Back to the Future* movies. Stricken at age thirty with Parkinson's disease, a disorder that destroys nerve cells, Fox took on a new role: activist for stem cell research that could cure his and other devastating diseases.

Stem cells taken from human embryos are like blank slates, able to create other cells that have specific jobs in the body, such as brain or muscle cells. This ability may lead to cures for cancer and heart disease. But using these cells destroys the embryo, and therein lies a controversy: Does harvesting stem cells kill a human being? Many people feel that destroying any human life, even at the cellular level, is murder.

George W. Bush opposed the harvesting of embryonic stem cells. He first restricted stem cell research in 2001. In 2006 he vetoed legislation that would allow researchers increased access to stem cells. At a press conference, Bush stated, "We must also remember that embryonic stem cells come from human embryos that are destroyed for their cells. Each of these human embryos is a unique human life with inherent dignity and matchless value." Standing beside Bush were twenty-four children who began life as embryos that, instead of being destroyed, were adopted by couples who could not have their own children.

While the debate over harvesting stem cells continues, people like Fox look toward stem cell research that may one day provide a cure for their disorders.

George W. Bush, "President Discusses Stem Cell Research Policy," press release, White House, July 19, 2006. http://georgewbush-whitehouse.archives.gov.

---

genes influence the processes of the body can help predict, treat, or even prevent disease. For that reason, scientists undertook a daunting task: to analyze human DNA and map the genome, or all the genes in the human body. It would be "a landmark in human history"[79] according to Dr. Robert Sinsheimer, who was instrumental in formulating the idea for the project.

In 1990 the international Human Genome Project (HGP), coordinated by the US Department of Energy and the National Institutes of Health, was established. Its goal, as set forth in its Five-Year Plan published in 1991, was no less than to change the future of biological science.

The information generated by the human genome project is expected to be the source book for biomedical science in the 21st century and will be of immense benefit to the field of medicine. It will help us to understand and eventually treat many of the more than 4000 genetic diseases that afflict mankind, as well as the many multifactorial diseases in which genetic predisposition plays an important role.[80]

Human DNA is so complicated that scientists estimated it would take fifteen years to complete the project. DNA can be thought of as a long, ladder-shaped molecule. Four chemicals, known as bases, join in pairs to make the ladder's rungs. There are about 3 billion of these base pairs in a human DNA molecule. Genes are segments of DNA that include base pairs in a certain order. The sequence in which they occur determines what a particular gene does. To unravel the secrets of the genome, scientists had to determine the order of the base pairs, a process known as sequencing. "Sequencing a gene is like reading a book one letter at a time to look for any spelling mistakes,"[81] commented Dr. David Miller from Boston Children's Hospital.

At the beginning, no one really knew how many genes the body contains: researchers estimated that there might be more than one hundred thousand. At HGP facilities in six countries, scientists began the laborious task of gene sequencing. After several years, progress remained steady but slow. For one man, it was too slow; he decided to take on the task of cracking the human genome by himself.

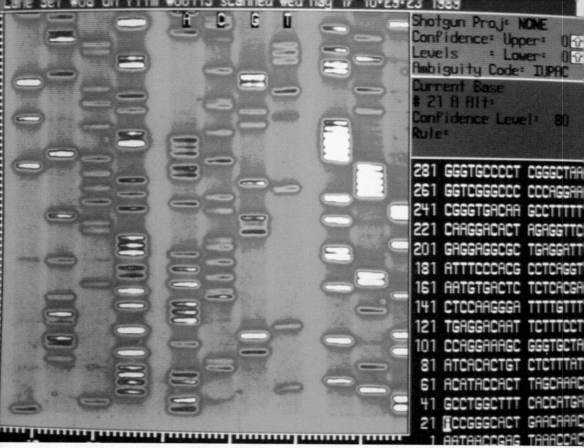

A computer image shows DNA sequencing of the human genome. The complete sequence of the human genome was published in 2003, allowing researchers to begin analyses that could lead to important advances in the biological and health sciences.

The Complete Human Map

J. Craig Venter was never one to follow the rules. After barely graduating from high school and enduring a stint in the navy that found him in jail twice, Venter eventually buckled down and received a PhD in physiology and pharmacology. He worked decoding brain-cell genes, using new, high-speed machinery and a sequencing technique that some colleagues felt produced inferior results. When Venter saw the slow progress of the HGP, he felt his system could obtain faster results. He formed a company named Celera Genomics and boasted that he could sequence the genome faster than the HGP. The race for the map of life was on.

Venter would later deny that he was "racing" against the HGP, saying, "To me, it's really a race to impact peoples' lives."[82] But the competition did spur the HGP to step up its game. Venter "stirred the pot,"[83] remarked Francis Collins, head of the HGP. The project streamlined its operation and even began using some of the latest computers and sequencing machines. But whether it was called a race or not, the end was a virtual tie. On June 26, 2000, President Bill Clinton stepped up to a podium in the White House. At his side were Collins and Venter. "We are here to celebrate the completion of the first survey of the entire human genome," said the president. "Without a doubt, this is the most important, most wondrous map ever produced by humankind."[84] But the scientists' work was not finished. The announcement referred to a "first draft" of the human genome, which was only about 90 percent complete. This draft, published in the science journal *Nature* in 2001, revealed that there are about 20,500 human genes, considerably fewer than previous estimates.

The complete sequence of the human genome was published in 2003. With this map, researchers could begin the long process of analyzing the genome to benefit the fields of biological and health sciences. One example of how this work might benefit people is Venter himself. He revealed that the genome Celera had sequenced was, in fact, his own, and that it showed he carried a gene that increased his risk of heart disease. This knowledge led him to adopt a healthier diet. Such information has the potential of saving countless others from deadly diseases.

The Mysteries of Mars

Eugene Cernan, the last man to walk on the moon, left his footprints in the dust of the lunar surface in 1972. Since that final Apollo lunar mission, no one has set foot on Earth's closest neighbor in space. After moon rocks and lunar photographs were analyzed, it seemed that the moon had given up all its secrets. But space held more mysteries to be solved, so scientists set their sights on a new challenge: Mars.

For decades, the Red Planet has been a popular setting in science fiction. Among the most famous stories was a 1938 radio broadcast of a Martian invasion of Earth that caused panic across America. Indeed, the possibility of life on Mars had been a tantalizing idea for years. One of the more radical theories suggested that the human race had descended from Martian space explorers who traveled to Earth eons ago. But scientific facts about Mars were even more enticing than fiction, and they raised a myriad of questions. Is there water on Mars? Could life have evolved on the planet? Sending astronauts to Mars to find the answers would be a formidable task. After an eight-month flight, they would encounter the hostile Martian environment, with its atmosphere of carbon dioxide and an average temperature of -81°F (-63°C). While it was not feasible to send a human to Mars, a robot would make an ideal Martian explorer.

Red Planet Rovers

In 2000 NASA approved a project to send two roving probes to Mars. Named *Spirit* and *Opportunity*, these six-wheeled robots could travel over the Martian surface, guided by engineers on Earth. They would take samples and photographs of the Martian landscape, much like a human scientist would do. Steven Squyres was the principal investigator for the Mars rover project. "I imagined sending a robot to Mars, a rolling geologist, with the hammers and drills and tools of a human geologist,"[85] he says. It took eight years to get his project funded, and three more to build and test *Spirit* and *Opportunity*. On June 10, 2003, *Spirit* was launched from Cape Canaveral, Florida. Less than a month later, on July 7, *Spirit*'s companion *Opportunity* lifted off toward Mars.

The most dangerous part of the flight was the landing. One malfunction and the $800 billion mission could be destroyed. On January 3, 2004, *Spirit* made a perfect touchdown on Mars and deployed its solar panels to power up its instruments and cameras. Soon pictures of the Martian surface were beaming back to Earth. "A beautiful horizon curves across the top of the scene," recalls Squyres. "Small dark rocks are scattered across the terrain. The resolution's low, so it's hard to say yet just what we're looking at. But we're sure not on Earth any more."[86] *Opportunity* landed on January 24, halfway across the planet from *Spirit*. The first pictures from *Opportunity* revealed that it had landed near a layered outcropping of Martian rock. Squyres called it "a martian history book, laid out right in front of us. We don't know how many pages there are, and we sure don't know what's written on them. But if we can figure this out, we'll have done what we came here to do."[87]

Spirit, *one of two NASA rovers that landed on Mars in 2004, uses its retractable arm to prepare and analyze rock samples from the planet's surface. The two rovers sent invaluable information and images to scientists back on Earth.*

The Search for Water

One of the things the rovers came to do was look for signs of water. *Spirit*'s first objective was a football-sized rock that scientists named Adirondack. Although *Spirit* only had to travel about 10 feet (3 m) to reach Adirondack, the journey took three days because of the rugged Martian terrain. *Spirit* drilled a hole in the rock and analyzed its composition with an instrument called an Alpha Particle X-ray Spectrometer. The rock was volcanic in nature, with no sign of water. Engineers then set *Spirit* on a course toward a ridge of hills about 1.5 miles (2.4 km) away. Meanwhile, scientists were studying the photographs of the layered rock *Opportunity* had landed near. They thought that the layers may have been created by an ancient flow of water. Some photographs showed small, round pebbles the scientists nicknamed blueberries, which may have been worn smooth by water. Chemical analysis of the blueberries by *Opportunity* revealed the presence of salts, which are often caused by evaporating water.

When *Spirit* reached the ridge, named Columbia Hills as a memorial to the Space Shuttle *Columbia* (which disintegrated during reentry in 2003, killing all crew members aboard), it uncovered numerous minerals there that indicated the former presence of water. One of these was goethite, a mineral that contains a component found in water. Squyres called the discovery "one more solid piece of evidence that water once flowed through those rocks."[88] Other indications that Mars once had water appeared at Meridiani Planum, a flat plain where *Opportunity* had landed. Photographs showed ripples in the Martian rocks. These appeared to have been formed either by water or by wind. After analyzing the pictures, scientists concluded that water, not wind, had caused the ripples. "We've nailed this thing,"[89] commented a jubilant rover project geologist.

Spirit and *Opportunity* had been designed to operate on the surface of Mars for about three months. But at the end of that period, the two hardy rovers were not about to quit. *Spirit* continued to explore until it got stuck in an area of soft Martian soil in May 2009. Efforts to free the rover were unsuccessful, and on May 25, 2011, its mission was officially ended, after more than seven years on Mars. As of June 2013, *Opportunity* was still going strong, thirty-eight times longer than the original three-month mission. Although *Spirit* and *Opportunity* encountered no Martians, their discoveries showed that conditions suitable for sustaining life existed on Mars at some point in its history. There is no evidence that Mars ever had life as advanced and varied as that found on Earth. But if primitive life such as bacteria once existed on the Red Planet, humans will eventually discover traces of such life, either by sending new robotic probes or by visiting the planet themselves.

Source Notes

Introduction: Milestones: A Measure of Progress

1. Quoted in Michael Preston and Kristen Kiraly, "Crews Finish Installing World Trade Center Spire," CNN, May 10, 2013. www.cnn.com.

Chapter One: A Changing Society

2. Quoted in Anita Hamilton, "100,000 Friends," *Time*, November 17, 2003. www.time.com.

3. Quoted in Candice M. Kelsey, *Generation MySpace*. New York: Marlowe, 2007, p. 1.

4. Quoted in Make a Difference for Kids, "Rachael's Story." www.makeadifferenceforkids.org.

5. Mark Zuckerberg Facebook page, October 4, 2012. www.facebook.com.

6. Quoted in David Sarno, "Twitter Creator Jack Dorsey Illuminates the Site's Founding Document, Part 1," *Technology* (blog), *Los Angeles Times*, February 18, 2009. http://latimesblogs.latimes.com.

7. Doug Gross, "Seven Years, Seven Lives Changed by Twitter," CNN, March 21, 2013. www.cnn.com.

8. Quoted in Jose Antonio Vargas, "The Face of Facebook," *New Yorker*, September 10, 2010. http://newyorker.com.

9. Quoted in *Guardian* (London), "Going Dutch: First Homosexual Weddings in Amsterdam," April 1, 2001. www.guardian.co.uk.

10. New American Standard Bible, Genesis 2:24, 2c ed., Lockman Foundation, 2013.

11. Quoted in Richard Lacayo, "Popping the Question," *Time*, December 1, 2003. www.time.com.

12. Quoted in Mariette le Roux, "World's First Legally Wed Couple Celebrates Their 10th Wedding Anniversary," News.com.au, March 30, 2011. www.news.com.au.

13. Quoted in Alia Malek, ed., *Patriot Acts: Narratives of Post-9/11 Injustice*. San Francisco: McSweeney's, 2011, p. 25.

14. Quoted in Malek, *Patriot Acts*, p. 46.

15. Quoted in Warren Richey and Linda Feldmann, "Has Post–9/11 Dragnet Gone Too Far?," *Christian Science Monitor*, September 12, 2003. www.csmonitor.com.

16. Quoted in Arab-American Anti-Discrimination Committee, "Anti-Arab Hate Crimes, Discrimination Continue—Killing in Detroit, Passengers Expelled from Airplanes," press release, September 21, 2001. www.adc.org

17. Quoted in Louise A. Cainkar, *Homeland Insecurity: The Arab American and Muslim American Experience After 9/11*. New York: Russell Sage Foundation, 2009, p. 207.

18. Quoted in Cainkar, *Homeland Insecurity*, p. 193.

19. Quoted in Walter V. Robinson, "For Father and Son, a Shared Anguish," *Boston Globe*, February 3, 2002. www.boston.com.

20. Thomas Plante, "A Perspective on Clergy Sexual Abuse," Psych Web, 2010. www.psychwww.com.

21. Quoted in Louise I. Gerdes, ed., *Child Sexual Abuse in the Catholic Church*. San Diego, Greenhaven, 2003, p. 15.

22. Quoted in Gerdes, *Child Sexual Abuse in the Catholic Church*, p. 15.

Chapter Two: Revolution in the Arts

23. Quoted in Karl Taro Greenfeld, Chris Taylor, and David E. Thigpen, "Meet the Napster," *Time*, October 2, 2000. www.time.com.

24. Quoted in Karl Taro Greenfeld, "The Free Juke Box," *Time*, March 27, 2000. www.time.com.

25. Stephen E. Siwek, "The True Cost of Sound Recording Piracy to the U.S. Economy," Institute for Policy Innovation, Policy Report 188, August, 2007. www.ipi.org.

26. Quoted in Thomas Mennecke, "Interview with a Victim of the RIAA," MP3Newswire.net, September 1, 2004. www.mp3news wire.net.

27. Quoted in David Goldman, "Music's Lost Decade: Sales Cut in Half," CNNMoney, February 3, 2010. http://money.cnn.com.

28. Quoted in Bernard Weinraub, "New Potter Book Casts Its Spell, and Promotional Wizardry Helps," *New York Times*, July 3, 2000. www .nytimes.com.

29. Quoted in David D. Kirkpatrick, "Harry Potter Magic Halts Bedtime for Youngsters," *New York Times*, July 9, 2000. www.nytimes .com.

30. Quoted in Holly Hartman, "With *Goblet* in Hand: Harry Potter Fans Celebrate Book Four," Infoplease, January 20, 2000. www.info please.com.

31. Quoted in Weinraub, "New Potter Book Casts Its Spell, and Promotional Wizardry Helps."

32. Quoted in Michael R. Walker, "A Teenage Tale with Bite," *BYU Magazine*, Winter 2007. www.magazine.byu.edu.

33. Lev Grossman, "Stephenie Meyer: A New J.K. Rowling?," *Time*, April 24, 2008. www.time.com.

34. Quoted in Jennie Yabroff, "Why Is It a Sin to Read for Fun?," *Daily Beast*, April 10, 2009. www.thedailybeast.com.

35. Quoted in John Anderson, "3-D Not an Alien Concept in Hollywood," *Arizona Republic*, March 26, 2009. www.azcentral.com.

36. Quoted in *Adrian Wooten,* "James Cameron—Part 2," *Guardian* (London), April 13, 2003. www.guardian.co.uk.

37. Quoted in Anderson, "3-D Not an Alien Concept in Hollywood."

38. Quoted in Ben Child, "James Cameron Takes 3D to China," *Guardian* (London), August 9, 2012. www.guardian.co.uk.

39. Taipei 101 Brochure, *Conception,* Taipei Financial Center Corporation, 2009. www.taipei-101.com.tw/en.

40. Quoted in Burj Khalifa, "Burj Khalifa's Grand Vision." www.burj khalifa.ae/en.

41. Quoted in *Architecture News*, "Burj Khalifa, Dubai—the World's Tallest Building," January 6, 2010. www.e-architect.co.uk.

Chapter Three: A Volatile Economy

42. Loren Fox, *Enron: The Rise and Fall*. Hoboken, NJ: Wiley, 2003, p. 221.

43. Quoted in Fox, *Enron*, pp. 361–362.

44. Quoted in Fox, *Enron*, p. 290.

45. Quoted in Lisa Prevost, "The Fallout of Subprime Loans," *New York Times*, July 15, 2007. www.nytimes.com.

46. George W. Bush, "President Calls for Expanding Opportunities to Home Ownership," White House, June 17, 2002. http://georgewbush-whitehouse.archives.gov.

47. Justin Fox, "Coping with a Real Estate Bust," *Time*, September 13, 2007. www.time.com.

48. Quoted in Edmund L. Andrews. "Fed Trims Its Forecast for Growth," *New York Times*, July 19, 2007. www.nytimes.com.

49. Quoted in Andrews, "Fed Trims Its Forecast for Growth."

50. Quoted in Mark Landler, "The U.S. Financial Crisis Is Spreading to Europe," *New York Times*, September 30, 2008. www.nytimes.com.

51. George W. Bush, "President Bush Addresses Nation," transcript, CNN, September 24, 2008. www.cnn.com.

52. Theodore Levitt, "The Globalization of Markets," *McKinsey Quarterly*, Summer 1984, p. 2. www.lapres.net.

53. Quoted in *Bloomberg Businessweek*, "China Is a Private-Sector Economy," August 21, 2005. www.businessweek.com.

54. Quoted in Robyn Meredith and Suzanne Hoppough, "Why Globalization Is Good," *Forbes*, April 16, 2007. www.forbes.com.

Chapter Four: Government and Politics

55. George W. Bush, "First Inaugural Address," White House, January 20, 2001. http://georgewbush-whitehouse.archives.gov.

56. George W. Bush, "Address to the Joint Session of the 107th Congress," White House, September 20, 2001. http://georgewbush-whitehouse.archives.gov.

57. United Nations Security Council, "United Nations Security Council Resolution 1373 (2001)," United Nations, September 28, 2001. www.un.org.

58. George W. Bush. *The National Security Strategy of the United States of America*, US Department of State, September 2002. www.state.gov.

59. George W. Bush, "Graduation Speech at West Point," White House, June 1, 2002. http://georgewbush-whitehouse.archives.gov.

60. Bush, *The National Security Strategy of the United States of America*.

61. Quoted in Thomas R. Mockaitis, *The Iraq War: A Documentary and Reference Guide*. Santa Barbara: Greenwood, 2012, p. 46.

62. Quoted in Steve Russell, "The Race to Capture Saddam," *Wall Street Journal*, December 3, 2011. http://online.wsj.com.

63. Quoted in Ewan MacAskill and Julian Borger, "Iraq War Was Illegal and Breached UN Charter, Says Annan," *Guardian* (London), September 15, 2004. www.guardian.co.uk.

64. Quoted in Richard Phillips with Stephan Talty, *A Captain's Duty*. New York: Hyperion, 2010, p. 106.

65. Quoted in Peter Eichstaedt, *Pirate State: Inside Somalia's Terrorism at Sea*. Chicago: Lawrence Hill, 2010, pp. 29–30.

66. Quoted in Voice of America, "Somali Piracy—Causes and Consequences," November 2, 2009. www.voanews.com.

67. Quoted in Voice of America, "Somali Piracy—Causes and Consequences."

68. Quoted in Richard Benedetto, "Address Throws Illinois' Obama into Whirlwind of Political Hopes," *USA Today*, July 27, 2004. www.usatoday.com.

69. Barack Obama, *The Audacity of Hope*. New York: Crown, 2006, p. 106.

70. Quoted in Christopher Wills, "Obama Learned from Failed Congress Run," *USA Today*, October 24, 2007. www.usatoday.com.

71. Barack Obama, "Presidential Announcement," Obama Speeches, February 10, 2007. http://obamaspeeches.com.

72. Barack Obama, "First Inaugural Address," White House, January 20, 2009. www.whitehouse.gov.

Chapter Five: Exploring New Frontiers

73. Quoted in Leander Kahney, "Straight Dope on the IPod's Birth," *Wired*. October 17, 2006. www.wired.com.

74. Quoted in Kahney, "Straight Dope on the IPod's Birth."

75. Quoted in in Walter Isaacson, *Steve Jobs*. New York: Simon & Schuster, 2011, p. 392.

76. Jared T. Miller, "The iPod Turns 10: How It Shaped Music History," *Time*, October 21, 2011. http://techland.time.com.

77. Quoted in Isaacson, *Steve Jobs*, p. 469.

78. Quoted in Isaacson, *Steve Jobs*, p. 474.

79. Quoted in Victor K. McElheny, *Drawing the Map of Life: Inside the Human Genome Project*. New York: Basic Books, 2010, p. 51.

80. National Institutes of Health, "Understanding Our Genetic Inheritance: The U.S. Human Genome Project," NIH Publication No. 90-1590, April 1990. www.ornl.gov.

81. Quoted in Bonnie Rochman, "*Time* Explains: Genome Sequencing," *Time*, October 22, 2012. http://healthland.time.com.

82. Quoted in Frederic Golden and Michael D. Lemonick, "The Race Is Over," *Time*, July 3, 2000, p. 23.

83. Quoted in Golden and Lemonick, "The Race Is Over," p. 22.

84. Quoted in James Shreeve, *The Genome War*. New York: Knopf, 2004, p. 356.

85. Quoted in Elizabeth Rusch, *The Mighty Mars Rovers: The Incredible Adventures of Spirit and Opportunity*. Boston: Houghton Mifflin Harcourt, 2012, p.13.

86. Steve Squyres, *Roving Mars: Spirit, Opportunity, and the Exploration of the Red Planet*. New York: Hyperion, 2005, p. 247.

87. Squyres, *Roving Mars,* p. 295.

88. Squyres, *Roving Mars,* p. 372.

89. Quoted in Squyres, *Roving Mars,* p. 320.

Important People: Cultural Milestones of the 2000s

Benedict XVI: Became head of the Roman Catholic Church in 2005. The priest sex abuse scandals took place while he was pope.

Ben Bernanke: The chair of the US Federal Reserve. He was criticized for not predicting the Great Recession and for approving corporate bailouts.

Osama bin Laden: The founder of the terrorist group al Qaeda, which sponsored terrorist attacks worldwide.

Tony Blair: The prime minister of the United Kingdom from 1997 to 2007. He was a staunch supporter of President George W. Bush's policies after the 9/11 attacks and during the Iraq War.

George W. Bush: The president of the United States from 2001 to 2009. He declared the War on Terror and signed the Emergency Economic Stabilization Act of 2008 into law.

James Cameron: The director of blockbuster movies such as *Titanic* and *Avatar*. He was a pioneer and vocal advocate of cutting-edge filmmaking techniques.

Francis Collins: The director of the Human Genome Project.

Shawn Fanning: The cofounder of Napster, the first music-sharing service on the Internet.

Hu Jintao: The president of the People's Republic of China from 2003 to 2013.

Saddam Hussein: The president of Iraq from 1979 to 2003. His regime was toppled during the Iraq War, and he was tried and executed for crimes against humanity.

Steve Jobs: The cofounder of Apple Computer (later renamed Apple Inc.). He was the creative force behind such revolutionary products as the Macintosh computer, the iPod, iPhone, and iPad.

Hamid Karzai: The president of Afghanistan. He took office in 2001 after the defeat of the Taliban regime.

Kenneth Lay: The chief executive officer of Enron Corporation. During his term as chief executive officer, accounting irregularities led to the collapse of the company. He was convicted of securities fraud but died before he could be sentenced.

Angela Merkel: Elected chancellor of Germany in 2005, the first woman to hold the office.

Stephenie Meyer: The author of the immensely popular *Twilight* series of vampire novels.

Barack Obama: The forty-fourth president of the United States. The first African American president, Obama was elected in 2008 and re-elected in 2012.

J.K. Rowling: The author of the *Harry Potter* book series. With the success of these novels, Rowling became the first billionaire author.

J. Craig Venter: Geneticist and founder of Celera Genomics. He competed with the Human Genome Project in the quest to sequence the human genome.

Mark Zuckerberg: The founder of Facebook. One of the most-visited websites on the Internet, Facebook revolutionized the concept of social networking.

Note: Below is a sampling of new words or words given new meaning during the decade, taken from a variety of sources.

bailout: Rescue by government of companies on the brink of failure.

birther: A person who believes that Barack Obama was not born in the United States and therefore cannot be president.

bling: Ostentatious displays of fortune and flash.

blog: A weblog.

chad: The tiny paper square that pops out when a voter punches the ballot card while casting a vote.

Chinglish: The growing Chinese-English hybrid language resulting from China's expanding influence.

click-through: Clicking on a banner ad on a website.

cloud computing: The practice of storing regularly used computer data on multiple servers that can be accessed through the Internet.

distracted driving: Multitasking while driving.

frenemy: Someone who is both friend and enemy.

generica: Strip malls, motel chains, prefab housing, and other features of the American landscape that are the same nationwide.

hacktivism: Activism by hackers.

hashtag: The # (hash) symbol used as a tag on Twitter.

helicopter mom/dad: A parent who micromanages his or her children's lives and is perceived to be hovering over every stage of their development.

locavore: Someone who cooks and eats locally grown food.

meh: Boring, apathetic, or unimpressive.

plutoed: To be demoted or devalued, as happened to the former planet Pluto.

push present: An expensive gift given to a woman by her husband in appreciation for having recently given birth.

red state/blue state: States whose residents predominantly vote Republican (red states) or Democrat (blue states).

same-sex marriage: Marriage of gay couples.

sandwich generation: People in their forties or fifties who are caring for young children and elderly parents at the same time.

sexting: Sending of sexually explicit text messages and pictures via cell phones.

snollygoster: A shrewd, unprincipled person; often used to refer to a politician.

staycation: A holiday spent at home and involving day trips to local attractions.

truthiness: Something one wishes to be the truth regardless of the facts.

tweet: To send a message via Twitter.

twixters: Adult men and women who still live with their parents.

unfriend: To remove someone from a friends list on a social networking site such as Facebook.

zombie bank: A financial institution kept alive only through government funding.

For Further Research

Books

Bryce G. Hoffman, *American Icon: Alan Mulally and the Fight to Save Ford Motor Company*. New York, Crown, 2012.

Walter Isaacson: *Steve Jobs*. New York: Simon & Schuster, 2011.

Stuart A. Kallen, *Technology 360: iPod and MP3 Players*. Detroit: Lucent, 2012.

Victor K. McElheny, *Drawing the Map of Life: Inside the Human Genome Project*. New York: Basic Books, 2010.

Barack Obama, *Dreams from My Father: A Story of Race and Inheritance*. New York: Crown, 2007.

Richard Phillips with Stephan Talty, *A Captain's Duty*. New York: Hyperion, 2010.

David Robson, *The Decade of the 2000s*. San Diego: ReferencePoint, 2012.

Elizabeth Rusch, *The Mighty Mars Rovers: The Incredible Adventures of Spirit and Opportunity*. New York: Houghton Mifflin Books for Children, 2012.

Mark Schultz, *The Stuff of Life: A Graphic Guide to Genetics and DNA*. New York: Farrar, Straus & Giroux, 2009.

Karen Sirvaitis, *Barack Obama: A Leader in a Time of Change*. Minneapolis: Twenty-First Century, 2010.

Websites

How Recessions Work (www.money.howstuffworks.com/recession2 .htm). Provides basic information on how the economy works, what recessions are, why they occur, and their effect on the economy.

Make a Difference for Kids (www.makeadifferenceforkids.org). Promotes the awareness of cyberbullying and suicide through education.

Marriage Equality USA (www.marriageequality.org). Advocates legally recognized civil marriage for all. Includes comprehensive facts and resources concerning same sex marriage.

Mars Exploration Rovers (http://marsrover.nasa.gov/home/index .html). NASA's Jet Propulsion Laboratory website contains extensive information about the Mars Rover project along with kids' activity pages and homework help.

Operation Iraqi Freedom (www.globalsecurity.org/military/ops/iraqi _freedom.htm). A comprehensive examination of the Iraq War, with links to facts about Iraq, a timeline, and major combat actions.

Pottermore (www.pottermore.com). Visitors to this site explore the *Harry Potter* books as an interactive experience.

Index

Note: Boldface page numbers indicate illustrations.

Craig E. Blohm has written numerous books and magazine articles for young readers. He and his wife, Desiree, reside in Tinley Park, Illinois.